The Perfect STORY PLOTTER

THE PLOT "ROBOT"

This is the mechanical unit of THE PLOT GENIE .. designed to serve the purpose of giving the writer or author a definite and arbitrary assignment of a number of elements comprising a plot outline which challenges the creative imagination and stimulates it to definite action by charting a course for it to pursue. The author-manipulator is urged to study the instructions in the Index Book carefully before attempting to use the Plot-Robot-Genie!

The Plot GENIE

Some Notes About This Edition

The Plot Genie Index was originally published in 1931 by The Gagnon Company in Hollywood, California.

The text of this book is taken from the *Plot Genie Supplemental Formula No. 3 Detective-Mystery* First edition 1933.

Hill referred to his cardboard spinner wheel as a "Plot Robot." An aspiring author was instructed to turn the device a certain number of times, to select a random number (usually between 1 to 180). *Plot Genie* users then consulted the lists to arrive at all the elements Hill believed necessary for a fully realized plot.

Bold Venture Press will have additional materials on its website for *Plot Genie* enthusiasts. A downloadable "Plot Robot," which can be assembled by eager authors, will be available. We are examining the possibility of offering professionally manufactured "Plot Robot" wheels for authors who prefer a more polished touch.

Several "Random Number Generators" are online. These websites make an excellent substitute for the Plot Robot.

Facsimile Edition
© 2015 Bold Venture Press.
All Rights Reserved.

"Plot Genie" and "Plot Robot" are
TM & © 2015 Bold Venture Press. All Rights Reserved.

ISBN-13: 978-1511696258
ISBN-10: 1511696257

www.boldventurepress.com

Bold Ventue Press edition May 2015

The Plot genie

DETECTIVE-MYSTERY

by
Wycliffe A. Hill
Author - Inventor

Supplementary
Formula No. 3

www.boldventurepress.com

A WORD FROM THE PUBLISHER

I believe that this special Supplementary Formula and Index for use with the "Plot Robot Genie" maintains the same high standard that has been established by the others of the series. It, too, should prove very popular with writers.

Detective-Mystery stories are always in demand for man has ever been intrigued by a mystery. This inherent desire to solve a puzzle is characteristic of everyone, irrespective of rank, creed, or class. In order to meet with the approval of editors and publishers, however, Detective-Mystery stories must have strong plots, an element of novelty, tense action, and more than the usual amount of suspense. The story plotted with this Formula will have all of these since the Index Book contains a wealth of plot elements or material which cannot help but produce desired results when compounded in the proper order.

In offering this book to the writing fraternity I feel that I am bringing to the desks of creative workers one of the most virile helps which has ever been devised.

While the "Plot Genie" has received the endorsement of some of the world's greatest writers, it is with extreme gratification that I learn of its extraordinary benefit to beginners.

I offer this Formula with the sincere hope that it will meet with the same gratifying success as has been accorded its predecessors.

Respectfully,

ERNEST E. GAGNON

INDEX

THE FORMULA

Plot Requisite	Genie Number	Suggestions from Index Book
The Crime Committed is		The Victim The Locale Type of crime
The Outstanding Clue is		
The Principal Suspects are		
The method of Investigation is		
A Suspicious Circumstance is		
A Thrilling Situation is		
The Solution is Precipitated by		
The Guilty one is		
Whose Motive was		

INTRODUCTION

It is with a great feeling of relief that I hand the finished manuscript for the Genie Formula and Index for Detective-Mystery to the publishers.

The compilation of this work has required many months involving a tremendous amount of research work, both on my part and on the part of an able staff of research workers supplied me by the publisher. We have endeavored to leave nothing undone that would provide those authors who use this work with every suggestion possible in the line of Detective-Mystery plot ideas. In fact, it is so complete that we believe that this Formula and Index is capable of supplying the plot outline for every Detective-Mystery story that ever has been written or ever will be written and that its manipulation would suggest any situation that could possibly occur, in connection with the commission of a murder, robbery, arson, forgery, or kidnapping, and the solution thereof.

The discovery of the Formula for the modern Detective-Mystery story was not difficult. It was the preparation of the Index, the editing of the material, its generalization in such a way that all desired latitude would be left to the imagination of the author, and its assembly in proper order, that has proven to be a monumental task.

Long before now, we realized that in order to make these Plot Genie Indices afford the maximum value to the author, the material which they contain must be susceptible to innumerable interpretations in the hands of various writers, in order that each may have ample opportunity to utilize or display his originality.

There are two members of my staff whose capable assistance and collaboration I desire to acknowledge. They are Miss Jane Sloan, head of the department and a very capable authoress and Miss Agnes Parsons, research worker. I hasten to admit also that in my study of Detective-Mystery, I received some interesting and valuable "slants" from the very excellent analysis of this type of story written by

Carolyn Wells, under the title of "The Technique of the Mystery Story", from the thrilling series written by Ashton-Wolfe in the American Weekly, and from witnessing many excellent photoplays, among which were "The Bishop Murder Case," "The Green Murder Case," "The Bat," "The Unholy Night," "Fu Manchu," and others.

WYCLIFFE A. HILL

THE DETECTIVE MYSTERY STORY

The modern detective-mystery story, in addition to being an interesting narrative, must have the added feature of being more or less of a guessing contest. In other words, the story and plot must be so constructed that the reader has an opportunity to match his wits with the detective or investigator, against the criminal, or against those of the detective in finding a solution of the crime.

Because they combine the excitement of the chase with the satisfaction of winning over an opponent in a game that requires mental activity, detective-mystery stories which deal with the hunting down of criminals have always been popular. There is the primeval instinct of a hunter in almost every man and we find it both thrilling and fascinating to watch and lie in wait and then suddenly pounce upon the quarry when it believes itself safe. It is a case of match cunning against cunning. The delight that men take in solving intricate puzzles is one of the vital manifestations of the law of nature, which demands a survival of the fittest. When mankind shall arrive at the summit of civilization and cease to crave for excitement or to take part in contests for superiority, before him will be only the down grade to mental and physical degeneracy..

Ashton-Wolfe, a member of the famous French Surete and whose articles have appeared in the American Weekly, has made some very interesting comments upon the writing of detective-mystery stories. He says: "There is at the present moment great interest in mystery-dramas on the stage and detective stories in fiction. It is an interesting fact that the super-human exploits of the famous detectives of fiction have had a profound influence upon the routine achievements of modern real life detectives—at least in some of the cities of Europe where technical scientific police laboratories and crime experts are maintained.

"Curiously enough, most writers of detective stories have manifested a decided preference for what has been termed analysis and deduction, and the immediate popularity of Sherlock Holmes was due chiefly to his super-ordinary ability to reconstruct a crime from insignificant details. For instance, in the 'Study of Scarlet', Holmes discovers a reactant which precipitates blood and nothing else and he distinguishes between arterial and venous blood. That, also, has become a distinct branch of criminal investigation. Poison, handwriting, stains, dust, footprints, traces of wheels, the shape and position of wounds, and therefore, the probable shape of the weapon which caused them, the basic principles of cryptograms—all these and many other excellent methods which germinated in Conan Doyle's fertile imagination, are now part and parcel of every detective's scientific equipment."

Ashton-Wolfe describes three methods of criminal investigation; the primitive system of spying and bribing men of the criminal class to become informers and betray their fellows; the science of tracking the criminal from the minute traces left by him on the scene of the crime and by his manner of operating, which to the trained observer is often as plain as a signature; and the classification of the various types of habitual lawbreakers which provides the certainty of recognizing a man or woman who has already been convicted, no matter how disguised and no matter under what alias he is hiding.

The first two of these methods may be employed in the writing of the modern detective-mystery story, but not the third, which applies to the apprehension of habitual criminals who do not play an important part, if any at all, in the type of detective-mystery stories which have proven to be the most popular.

The reader should bear in mind that there is a decided difference between the so-called true detective story, which is usually an elaboration on facts, and the detective-mystery story of today. In the latter, with which this Index deals, the principal characters, victims, as well as criminals, are people of importance and the background is colorful. The criminal or guilty person should be one who would not be ordinarily suspected of the commission of a crime. The motives and methods should be unusual and difficult to detect and there should be involved in the plot a number of suggested sub-plots, all of which naturally introduce themselves with the multiplicity of suspects. The motives and methods of the natural or professional criminal are as a rule too well known to be interesting. So are the methods employed in their detection.

Bertillion, the famous French detective who originated the finger-print system, propounded what he called the Rule of Three when in search of a motive for the commission of a crime. It was:

1. Who profits by the crime?
2. Find the woman.
3. Seek the motive.

The first two are more easily answered than the last.

I classify all motivation under three heads. They are:

1. The desire to possess.
2. The desire for relief.
3. The desire for revenge.

In other words, one wants to get something, get rid of something, or get even with somebody—to use a colloquialism.

The three methods of criminal investigation described by Ashton-Wolfe must be elaborated upon in the detection of the super-criminal whom we find in the modern popular detective-mystery story. That is, by the use of strategy. In other words, one of the most interesting methods employed by the modern detective or investigator is the setting of some kind of a trap which causes the criminal to disclose himself. The manner in which he does this or the novelty employed not only adds interest to the story, but intensifies the suspense in the mind of the reader or observer, who reads or watches with anxiety to see whether or not the strategy employed by the detective or investigator is going to be successful. The reader may even be kept in the dark and mystified as to what the intentions of the detective are in order to heighten the effect.

In the list of "Methods", one of the plot elements included in this Formula and appearing in this Index, we have included a great many which will provide interesting suggestions for the use of strategy in the search for a solution of the crime.

The author of the modern detective-mystery story must have a certain amount of inventive genius, or be familiar with modern inventions and branches of knowledge, tools, or mechanisms which he may place in the hands of his criminals and with which he must also equip his detective. In fact, the detective should be in possession of more vital knowledge and efficient weapons than the criminal, if one is going to arm the two of them with such paraphernalia. A conflict that is one-sided is never interesting, however, so it would not do to endow either side with all of the advantage.

BASIC RULES

The plot of the modern detective-mystery story may be briefly described as follows: A crime is committed; although evidence is discovered which points to several persons as the guilty ones, the solution appears exceedingly difficult. No motive is apparent. The victim is a respectable, well-to-do person of importance, but not necessarily a sympathetic character. A detective or investigator, usually not a member of the police department, is called in and he immediately establishes a surveillance over a number of suspects. The reader is made aware of the fact that the detective suspects these several persons and is started to guessing by what appears to be the suspicious actions of several of those who are suspected. Baffling circumstances follow, which may either deceive the detective and the reader and throw them completely off the track temporarily or in which the reader may be deceived or mystified by the methods employed by the detective. In the meantime, in addition to the crime already committed, another more serious one perhaps impends and it is up to Mr. Detective to apprehend the clever criminal before disastrous consequences develop. As the climax is approached, evidence must point strongly every minute to the real criminal, as one by one the other suspects, who should be more or less sympathetic characters, are absolved and a logical explanation given for their previous apparently suspicious actions. Then, there is a thrilling capture of the real criminal, who should prove to be also a person of importance and one who would not ordinarily be suspected of committing such a crime. If the motive of the criminal, when disclosed, proves to be a strange one, novelty is added to the story.

The author should regard the writing of a detective-mystery story in the light of a game or sporting event and should not trick or deceive the reader. On the other hand, he must outwit the reader ingeniously and give him an equal opportunity with the detective in solving the mystery. There should be no hidden clues known to the detective only, but all of them should be plainly stated and described. Only such tricks and deceptions as are played legitimately by the criminal on the detective may be played on the reader.

The criminal or guilty person should not be a surprise character who is brought into the story at the last, but should be one who has played a more or less prominent part in the story from the beginning. In other words, he should be a person with whom the reader is familiar and in whom he takes an interest.

There should be only one detective and only one criminal. The latter may, of course, have a number of accomplices among whom there may be, if desired, professional criminals or members of the underworld. It should never develop that the detective himself is the criminal because that would be outright trickery and deception of the reader.

The solution of the crime should also be found by logical deduction or by the clever efforts of the detective and not by mere accident or coincidence. Neither should the criminal be permitted to make a voluntary confession, which is unmotivated. Such action would spoil the climax.

The crime or problem which is to be solved should also be of such a logical nature that it is always apparent if the reader is shrewd enough to see it. In other words, should he re-read the story, he should be able to say to himself, "It is very plain who committed the crime. Why didn't I see that before?" The plot of the detective-mystery story must of necessity be more or less mechanical and it should contain no long descriptions or character sketches, which hold up the action and detract attention from the main purpose, which is as S. S. Van Dine puts it, "To state a problem, analyze it, and bring it to a successful conclusion."

Love interest, if introduced at all in the detective-mystery story, should be subordinated. The problem in a story of this kind is not to enable a couple to remove the obstacles to their love, but to bring a criminal to the bar of justice. Therefore, love interest should be merely incidental. The author is no better than a practical joker who writes a detective-mystery story in which the crime turns out to be an accident or a suicide. There must have been a real crime committed, backed by a powerful motive.

NOT ALL MURDER STORIES

Detective-mystery stories do not necessarily all deal with a murder. It has been discovered that one-half of all detective stories are murder stories, one-fourth are robberies, and the other one-fourth are such miscellaneous wrongdoings as forgery, counterfeiting, blackmail, arson, dynamiting, and body-snatching. We have classified these minor crimes under four heads, as follows: Robbery, forgery, destruction of property, and kidnapping, and in the general directions which are to be found on another page, the reader will find complete instructions how to proceed, if he desires to use this Formula and Index to plot a detective-mystery story which deals with some crime other than murder.

Of course, the most interesting and perhaps the most salable are those detective-mystery stories which deal with the proposition of murder. The victim is usually dead when the story begins, unless the problem may be a matter of preventing a crime. In any event, the identity of the criminal, disclosed at the last, must be the greatest surprise in the story.

A great deal depends on the setting in the writing of a detective story which deals with one of the four crimes other than murder. For instance, a robbery must be made interesting by unusual characters and conditions and the booty should be of great importance or value. Disgrace and disaster of the worst kind must threaten the discovery of the guilty party. The motive in such a crime must be very picturesque and interesting and not merely the desire to possess things of ordinary value or to obtain revenge against an insignificant offender.

The manner in which a detective-mystery story is told or presented is as important as the plot itself. The author must know how his story is going to end but he should be very careful not to tip this to the reader. The type of story with which we are dealing here depends largely on action, excitement, thrills, suspense. The attention of the reader must be arrested, his curiosity aroused, and his interest awakened at the very start. Suspense must be maintained throughout the story and the final explanation must more than satisfy his anticipation. A detective-mystery story which is well-written should leave the reader in a more or less reflective mood with an abundance of food for thought, but with no questions which have not been satisfactorily answered.

SAMPLE PLOTS

We are now going to dial out ten sample plots of Detective-Mystery stories and choose one of them for further development. Following each outline, we will write a short synopsis and generalize these in such a way that a great deal of latitude will be left to the imagination of the author.

Although it is suggested in the special instructions which precede the list of story elements further along, that the author may determine for himself how many elements he is to use from certain of the lists, we have arbitrarily decided to use the following formula in these sample plots.

Operation 1—Dial 3 Elements
Operation 2—Dial 2 Elements
Operation 3—Dial 3 Elements
Operation 4—Dial 2 Elements
Operation 5—Dial 3 Elements
Operation 6—Dial 1 Element
Operation 7—Dial 1 Element
Operation 8—Dial 1 Element
Operation 9—Dial 1 Element

The following are the outlines and the Thumb-nail Synopsis which has been developed from each. I want to emphasize the fact that it is very important, as soon as the author has obtained the desired outline, that he proceed to write the Thumb-nail Synopsis as I have done here. He will find that this will assist materially in the first step toward cementing together the various story elements which in the outline itself may appear at first glance to be contradictory, or to have no possible relationship. As soon as this Thumb-nail Synopsis has been written, he may then discard the outline altogether before proceeding further.

I

1. The crime committed is—

143—Victim—An international spy.

91—Locale—In India.

40—Type of Crime—Two small red marks are found on throat.

2. The outstanding clue is—

103—Evidence of a struggle.

52—A scrawl on paper or on anything else.

3. The principal suspects are—

58—A society girl.

120—A circus barker.

9—An employee.

4. Method of investigation.

129 (1) An affinity is traced.

25 (2) A sensational expose is planned.

5. Suspicious and baffling circumstances are—

135 (2) A peculiar assortment of objects has been concealed and is discovered.

140 (2) A person who usually retired early is discovered prowling.

88 (3) Attempt to remove or conceal bloodstains is discovered.

6. A thrilling situation develops

151—There is a threatened murder of a friend of the victim.

7. The solution is precipitated by—

99—The criminal is identified when a note written by the victim comes to light.

8. The guilty person is—

103—An autocrat.

9. Whose motive was

110 (1) To emphasize a protest or serve as an example.

THUMB NAIL SYNOPSIS

The locale of this story is in India. It is a murder story and the body of a man or woman is found with two small red marks on the throat. The outstanding clue in addition to the evidence of a fierce struggle is a scrawl on a piece of paper, which is found near by. Suspected of the crime are three people—a society girl, a circus barker, and an employee. An investigator is called upon the scene and he puts into operation two methods in an effort to solve the crime. One of these is the tracing of an affinity, who may be of the victim, the guilty person, or someone else. The other is a plan to precipitate an expose which will throw some light on the crime. Among the suspicious and baffling circumstances which develop are these—there is discovered a peculiar assortment of objects which have been concealed; a person who usually retired early is observed to be prowling at night and there is also discovered an attempt to remove or conceal bloodstains. A thrilling situation develops when there is a threatened murder of a friend of the victim. Finally, the criminal comes to light and it develops that the guilty person is an autocrat and that his motive was to emphasize a protest of some kind or serve as an example. The victim is identified as an international spy.

II

1. The crime committed is
        59—A female mystic.
        61—On a houseboat.
        125—A pistol shot in the ear.
2. The outstanding clue is
        131—An incomplete inscription.
        79—A surgical instrument.
3. The principal suspects are
        85—An hypnotic subject.

91—A pagan priest.

96—A stickler for a tradition.

4. Method of investigation is

    159 (1) Modern science is employed.

    170 (2) There is a reconstruction of the crime for effect.

5. Suspicious and baffling circumstances are

    107 (2) A secreted manuscript comes to light.

    170 (2) It is discovered that a picture or motion picture has been taken.

    176 (3) A person turns berserk over a question, accusation, or incident.

6. A thrilling situation develops

    7—There is an outburst of emotion.

7. The solution is precipitated by

    127—The discovery of secret panels, concealed places of entrance and exit, underground tunnels, etc., which lead to the capture of the criminals.

8. The guilty person is

    75—A manufacturer.

9. Whose motive was

    80 (3) To escape the necessity of giving an answer.

THUMB NAIL SYNOPSIS

The body of a woman is found on a houseboat. The woman has been murdered by a pistol shot in the ear. The outstanding clues are the presence of a surgical instrument and an incomplete inscription which are found near the body. The principal suspects are an hypnotic subject, a pagan priest, and a stickler for a tradition. The method of investigation which is adopted by the detective is the reconstruction of the crime for effect and the employment of modern science. Suspicious and baffling circumstances which develop are three in number. A secreted manuscript comes to light. It is discovered that a picture or a motion picture has been taken. In addition to this, a person turns berserk over a question, accusation, or incident and there is an outburst of emotion. The solution is precipitated by the discovery of secret panels, concealed places of entrance and exit, or an underground tunnel and this leads to the capture of the criminal. It develops that the murderer is a manufacturer who has committed the crime in order to escape the necessity of giving an answer. The woman victim is a female mystic.

III

1. The crime committed is
      56—A missionary.
      2—In a bank.
      13—A pistol shot in the body.
2. The outstanding clue is
      86—Evidence pointing to revenge.
      93—A utensil.
3. The principal suspects are
      46—One who has been accused by the victim.
      56—A fortune teller.
      146—An ex-employee.
4. Method of investigation is
      25 (1) There is an adulteration of material, matter, or liquid.
      173 (2) Investigator impersonates a criminal to secure information.
5. Suspicious and baffling circumstances are
      107 (1) Saving of a life interfered with.
      178 (1) The credentials of an important character are stolen.
      20 (3) Unexpected discovery of the illegitimacy of a child.
6. A thrilling situation develops
      151—There is a threatened murder of a friend of the victim.
7. The solution is precipitated by

165—It is discovered that a suspect has the characteristics of a sadist.

8. The guilty person is
120—An animal fancier.

9. Whose motive was
2 (1) To escape from abdication or banishment.

THUMB NAIL SYNOPSIS

In this case, the murder takes place in a bank. The victim is a missionary who has been shot with a pistol. Evidence is produced to show that the man had enemies who sought revenge and discovered near the scene of the crime is a utensil. The principal suspects are one who has been accused by the victim, a fortune teller, and an ex-employee. The detective or investigator sets about to solve the crime by using two methods. One of these is an adulteration of material, matter, or liquid and the other is that he impersonates a criminal to secure information. Suspicious and baffling circumstances are introduced when the saving of a life is interfered with, the credentials of an important character are stolen, and there is a discovery of the illegitimacy of a child. A thrilling situation follows in which there is a threatened murder of a friend of the victim. The solution is approached with the discovery that one of the suspects has the characteristics of a sadist and that the guilty person is an animal fancier, whose motive was to escape from abdication or banishment.

IV

1. The crime committed is
78—A botanist.
38—In a dark hallway.
169—Suffocation by garroting.

2. The outstanding clue is
10—Evidence that the victim had practiced deception.

83—An envelope or paper.
3. The principal suspects are
        97—A Chinese.
        54—The loser in a game.
        8—A witness.
4. The method of investigation is
        78 (1) An unknown lover or sweetheart is sought.
        53 (1) A suspect is lead to believe that another suspect has confessed.
5. Suspicious and baffling circumstances are
        38 (1) An old legend is described as having a bearing on the case.
        116 (1) A humorous accusation or statement proves to be serious.
        134 (1) A drink is discovered to contain liquor or poison.
6. A thrilling situation develops
        96—There is a panic.
7. The solution is precipitated by
        111—The criminal, believing everything to be lost, makes a voluntary confession.
8. The guilty person is
        123—A doctor.
9. Whose motive was
        135 (2) The ambition to gain wealth or fame.

THUMB NAIL SYNOPSIS

The body of a botanist is found in a dark hallway and the man or woman has been killed by suffocation or garroting. A clue is supplied when it is known that the victim has practiced deception on another and there is also found near the body an envelope or paper which is significant. Suspected of the crime are a Chinese, the loser in a game, and the witness. The investigator sets about to solve the crime by seeking the unknown lover or sweetheart. He also attempts to lead a suspect to believe that an accomplice has confessed. Baffling and suspicious circumstances develop in which an old legend is described as having a bearing on the case, a humorous accusation or statement proves to be serious, and a drink is discovered to contain liquor or poison. A thrilling situation develops when there is a panic and the criminal, believing everything to be lost, makes a voluntary confession. The guilty person is a doctor, whose motive was his ambition to gain wealth and fame.

V

1. The crime committed is
      133—A contractor.
      34—At a mill.
      106—The use of a mechanical device.
2. The outstanding clue is
      62—Evidence that the victim has balked someone's plans.
      134—A half-emptied glass or dish.
3. The principal suspects are
      34—A medium.
      105—A spy.
      119—A rival in business.
4. Method of investigation is
      73 (2) A situation of chaos is perpetrated.
      46 (2) An apparition is employed.
5. Suspicious and baffling circumstances are
      93 (1) An attempt to conceal apparel.
      168 (1) An attempt has been made to throw away some object which supposedly has some bearing on the case.
      8 (3) Insistent declaration of alibi by suspect.
6. A thrilling situation develops
      18—There is an embarrassing discovery.
7. The solution is precipitated when

32—Rivals come face to face and each accuses the other
of the crime.
8. The guilty person is
160—An hypnotist.
9. Whose motive was
60 (1) Because of excessive grief.

THUMB NAIL SYNOPSIS

The locale of this story is in or about a mill and the victim is a
contractor who has been killed by the use of a mechanical device.
Evidence develops that the victim has balked someone's plans and
discovered near the body is a half-emptied glass or dish. The principal suspects are a medium, a spy, and a rival in business. In an
attempt to solve the murder, the investigator perpetrates a situation
of chaos or confusion and an apparition is caused to appear. Suspicious and baffling circumstances are an attempt to conceal wearing
apparel, an effort to throw away some object which supposedly has
some bearing on the case and the insistent declaration of an alibi by
a suspect. A thrilling situation develops when there is an embarrassing discovery. The solution is precipitated when the rivals come face
to face and each accuses the other of the crime. It develops that the
guilty person is an hypnotic or one who is interested in hypnotism
and he was driven to commit the crime because of excessive grief.

VI

1. The crime committed is
14—A bon vivant.
83—At a spiritualistic hall.
96—A small puncture at the base of the brain.
2. The outstanding clue is
110—Evidence that the victim was engaged in a propaganda
campaign.

7—A badge, medal, decoration.
3. The principal suspects are
134—An adventurer.
145—A delivery man.
44—A disguised person.
4. Method of investigation is
114 (2) Evidence of the presence of a maniac is traced.
7 (1) A woman in the case is sought.
5. Suspicious and baffling circumstances are
131 (2) A person is fawning or obsequious to another.
37 (2) The discovery of the concealment of evidence of antagonism.
54 (2) A person unexpectedly shows undue anxiety.
6. A thrilling situation develops
72—A plot or device to frighten is discovered.
7. The solution is precipitated when
87—Mental telepathy is used in the solution of the crime.
8. The guilty person is
45—An author.
9. Whose motive was
174 (1) The anxiety to remove necessary evidence.

THUMB NAIL SYNOPSIS

The victim in this story is a bon vivant, whose body is discovered in a spiritualistic hall. There is a small puncture at the base of the brain. Evidence is discovered that the victim was engaged in a propaganda campaign and also on his body is found a badge, medal, or decoration. The principal suspects are an adventurer, a delivery man, and a disguised person. The method of investigation employed by the detective is the tracing of evidence of the presence of a maniac and also a woman is sought in the case. Suspicious and baffling circumstances develop in which it is observed that a person is fawning or obsequious to another for an unexplainable reason, the discovery of the concealment of evidence of antagonism and the unexpected exhibition of undue anxiety of a character. A thrilling situation develops with the discovery of a plot or device intended to frighten. Mental telepathy is used in the solution of the crime and the guilty person proves to be an author whose motive was to remove necessary evidence.

VII

1. The crime committed is
   176—A sculptor.
   74—In a logging camp.
   32—The head is battered in with a blunt instrument.
2. The outstanding clue is
   163—The evidence of a peculiar means of escape.
   179—A search warrant.
3. The principal suspects are
   78—A wealthy delinquent.
   151—A voodoo doctor.
   109—One who is suspected of conspiracy.
4. Method of investigation is
   118 (1) Burglary is committed or planned.
   175 (1). A clandestine meeting is spied upon.
5. Suspicious and baffling circumstances are
   80 (3) A person resents an examination.
   158 (3) Discovery that a person has been threatened with prosecution.
   58 (2) A legatee is unexpectedly produced or discovered.
6. A thrilling situation develops
   127—A mysterious method of disposing of the corpse is discovered.
7. The solution is precipitated by
   7—Criminal is permitted to escape when it develops that he or she is a loved one.

8. The guilty person is
      95—A radio announcer.
9. Whose motive was
      167 (3) Vengeance against a robber.

THUMB NAIL SYNOPSIS

This story takes place in or about a logging camp. The body of a sculptor is found with the head battered in by a blunt instrument. Outstanding clues are the discovery of evidence of a peculiar means of escape and of a search warrant near the body. The principal suspects are a wealthy delinquent, a voodoo doctor, and one who is suspected of conspiracy. The methods of investigation employed by the detective are the commission of a burglary and the spying upon a clandestine meeting. Suspicious and baffling circumstances develop when a person resents an examination, the discovery is made that a person has been threatened with prosecution and it is learned that a legatee has unexpectedly been produced. A thrilling situation develops with the discovery of a mysterious method of plotting to dispose of the corpse. The crime is solved with the discovery that the guilty person is a radio announcer, a loved one who is permitted to escape. His motive was vengeance against a robber.

VIII

1. The crime committed is
      40—A gambler.
      106—In the forest.
      4—Cutting the throat.
2. The outstanding clue is
      76—The presence of a mysterious device.
      90—Merchandise.
3. The principal suspects are
      162—A lover of wife or beloved of husband.

117—A passerby.
130—An heir or an heiress.
4. Method of investigation is
146 (2) An appeal is made to conceit.
98 (1) The connection of a Hindu is investigated.
5. Suspicious and baffling circumstances are
50 (1) Giving out the wrong address.
10 (2) A person's credentials proved false.
31 (2) A person is found to be mentally deficient or delinquent.
6. A thrilling situation develops
40—There is a trail by bloodhounds.
7. The solution is precipitated when
1—There is a thrilling pursuit and capture.
8. The guilty person is
129—A dramatic critic.
9. Whose motive was
84 (3) To investigate supernaturalism.

THUMB NAIL SYNOPSIS

The body of a gambler is found in the forest with throat cut. The outstanding clues are the presence of a mysterious device and a quantity of merchandise. The principal suspects are a lover of wife or beloved of husband, a passerby, and an heir or an heiress. The methods of investigation employed by the detective are an appeal that is made to conceit and the investigation of the connection of a Hindu. Suspicious and baffling circumstances develop when a wrong address is given out, a person's credentials prove to be false and a person is found to be mentally delinquent or deficient. A thrilling situation develops when there is a trail by bloodhounds. There is a thrilling pursuit and capture of the criminal, who proves to be a dramatic critic, whose motive was to investigate supernaturalism.

IX

1. The crime committed is
    131—A judge.
    145—On a ferry boat.
    158—A shotgun wound in the mouth.
2. The outstanding clue is
    173—The custodian of the victim's valuables is assaulted, and events prove the action was premeditated.
    16—A jewel.
3. The principal suspects are
    32—An apparition.
    47—A partner.
    1—A job seeker.
4. Method of investigation is
    16 (1) Shadowing.
    52 (1) A prisoner is apparently given his freedom and his movements are watched.
5. Suspicious and baffling circumstances are
    90 (3) An effort to bully or brow-beat comes to light.
    111 (2) A person is discovered keeping an appointment after attempting to conceal his plans.
    132 (2) Report of an unusual sound or noise is revealed.
6. A thrilling situation develops when
    151—There is a threatened murder of a friend of the victim.
7. The solution is precipitated by
    50—A friend in disguise saves the day for the innocent suspect and identifies the criminal.
8. The guilty person is
    61—A captain.
9. Whose motive was
    76 (1) Jealous revenge.

THUMB NAIL SYNOPSIS

The victim in this story is a judge and the body is found aboard a ferry boat with a shot gun wound in the mouth or face. Outstanding clue is that the custodian of the victim's valuables is assaulted and events prove the action was premeditated. A valuable jewel is found on or near the body. The principal suspects are an apparition, a partner and a job seeker. The methods of investigation employed by the detective are shadowing and also apparently giving his freedom to a prisoner and then watching his movements. Suspicious and baffling circumstances develop when an effort to bully or browbeat comes to light, a person is discovered keeping an appointment after attempting to conceal his plans and the report of an unusual noise or sound is revealed. A thrilling situation develops when there is a threatened murder of a friend of the victim. The solution is precipitated when a friend in disguise saves the day for an innocent suspect and identifies the criminal who develops to be a captain whose motive was jealous revenge.

X

1. The crime committed is
    1.—A politician.
    174—At a seance.
    129—A scratch from a poisoned thorn.
2. The outstanding clue is
    86—Evidence pointing to revenge.
    100—A bone or bones.
3. The principal suspects are
    115—A sub-contractor.
    68—A sales person.
    140—A promoter.
4. Method of investigation is

155 (2) An enigma is offered.

21 (1) The past of a character is investigated.

5. Suspicious and baffling circumstances are

112 (3) A message is found to be a ruse or decoy.

124 (1) A suspected person attempts to conceal a hurt or a wound, or destroy evidence of how it was done.

137 (3) It is revealed that there has been a controversy over religious questions.

6. A thrilling situation develops

72—A plot or device to frighten is discovered.

7. The solution is precipitated when

144—It develops that a suspect has been connected with some previous crime.

8. The guilty person is

44—A sportsman.

9. Whose motive was

19 (2) Vengeance against one who has brought disgrace and ruin.

THUMB NAIL SYNOPSIS

A murder is committed at a spiritualistic seance. The victim is a politician who is murdered mysteriously. Evidence points to revenge sought by enemies and there is discovered near by a bone or bones. The principal suspects are a sub-contractor, a sales person and a promoter. The investigator hits on the idea of propounding an enigma and of investigating the past of a character. Suspicious and baffling circumstances develop when a message is found to be a ruse or decoy, a suspected person attempts to conceal a hurt or a wound or to destroy evidence of how it was done and it is revealed that there has been a controversy over religious questions. A thrilling situation develops with the discovery of a plot or device which is designed to cause fright. It develops that a suspect has been connected with some previous crime, and that the guilty person is a sportsman who seeks vengeance against one who has brought disgrace or ruin. In the end, it is discovered that death resulted from the scratch of a poisoned thorn.

We have decided to choose No. 4 in the further development of a plot from the thumb-nail synopsis which follows the outline, although there are several others which appear to be equally promising.

The next step in the process of development is to ask ourselves a number of questions concerning HOW these things could be after GENIE tells us WHAT hppens. When we have found satisfactory answers to these questions the plot will be materially developed. The questions in this case might be as follows:

1. Is the botanist a man or a woman?
   A—A man.
2. In what building is the hallway where the body is found?
   A—Laboratory.
3. Why is the victim garroted instead of being killed in some other way?
   A—To conceal the mark of a poisoned hypodermic.
4. How was the victim garroted and with what?
   A—With a silk scarf.
5. What evidence is discovered to show that the victim had practiced deception on someone?
   A—A note in Chinese to the botanist.
6. On whom was the deception practiced?
   A—A Chinese.
7. What is contained in or on the envelope or paper found near the body?
   A—A protest from a Chinese against the botanist's failure to divide profits.
8. Why is suspicion thrown on the Chinese?
   A—Because of the note.

9. Who is the Chinese and what relationship does he bear to the botanist?

A—An old herb-doctor.

10. Who is the person who has lost money in a game?

A—A young spendthrift member of an aristocratic family.

11. Who is the witness?

A—An old peg-leg negro servant.

12. What did he witness?

A—He witnessed a quarrel between the botanist and the rich young man.

13. Why did the detective or investigator make a search for an unknown sweetheart?

A—Following up the clue in the shape of the silk scarf.

14. Who is the unknown sweetheart?

A—A notorious woman—a member of the demi-monde.

15. What suspect is approached by the detective with the claim that an accomplice has confessed?

A—The old negro, to make it appear that the young man has confessed.

16. Is the attempt successful?

A—No.

17. What old legend is described as having a bearing on the case?

A—One that is described by the old negro wherein a certain dream that he has presages a death in the family.

18. What character believes in the legend and suggests it in connection with the mystery?

A—The old negro.

19. Who makes the humorous accusation or statement which later on proves to be serious?

A—The demi-mondaine.

20. To whom is the statement made?
    A—The doctor.
21. In whose presence is the statement made?
    A—The maid.
22. Who discovers a drink which contains poison?
    A—The maid.
23 Where is it discovered?
    A—In the apartment of the demi-mondaine.
24. Does anyone take the poison?
    A—No.
25. If not, what prevents it?
    A—The maid, a drug addict, removes it to protect the
    doctor.
26. What kind of a panic is precipitated at or near the
    climax?
    A—A panic is precipitated by a raid on the doctor's of-
    fice by several supposedly-demented drug addicts.
    The raid is staged by the detectives.
27. Where does the panic occur?
    A—At the doctor's office.
28. What leads the criminal to believe that everything is
    lost and causes him to make a voluntary confession?
    A—Confronted with evidence that the demi-mondaine
    has confessed and accused him.
29. Who is the murderer?
    A—The doctor.
30. What is his motive?
    A—Desire for wealth.
31. What becomes of him?
    A—He commits suicide. In his confession he illustrates
    to the detective how he administered the hypodermic
    to the botanist and then suddenly pierces his own
    throat and so dies.

SYNOPSIS

The body of a botanist or scientist is discovered in a dark hallway in his laboratory building. He has apparently been suffocated by garroting and around his neck is a silk scarf. Among his papers is found a note written in Chinese, which upon being deciphered, proves to be a protest from an old Chinese herb-doctor against a swindle which has been perpetrated upon him by the botanist in connection with a split on the proceeds on a certain mysterious herb that has been discovered by the botanist with the aid of the Chinese. The Chinese is naturally suspected as the murderer.

The body of the botanist has been discovered by an old negro servant—a peg-leg who is very superstitious. The negro is also suspected when he insists on describing an old legend which presages death in the family following a peculiar dream he claims to have had. The old servant is suspected of being more or less demented.

When the old negro discovers the body he rushes out and calls to a doctor who has just driven up and is about to enter the place. The old servant knows the doctor to be a friend of the botanist and a business associate of some kind.

The botanist is known to be a frequent visitor of a certain high class gambling club and among his friends and associates is a young spendthrift and bon-vivant who is a member of a highly respected family. He also gambles and the investigator learns that this man has recently lost heavily at the gambling table while the botanist has been a winner. It is learned that a large sum of money which has been won by the botanist has recently disappeared from his safe and this throws suspicion on the young spendthrift.

The presence of the silk scarf around the victim's neck causes the detective to make a search for the owner who proves to be a demi-mondaine with whom the botanist is infatuated.

Employed by this woman is a maid who, because she is addicted to the use of the drug which the doctor is dispensing and being dependent upon him for it, remains silent although she suspects him of attempting to poison her mistress.

The detective grills this girl and forces her to tell how she had overheard the demi-mondaine jokingly accuse the doctor of committing the murder some days before.

The young spendthrift is absolved of the crime when the detective discovers through the girl that a large sum of money has been given the demi-mondaine by the botanist and this accounts for the disappearance of the money from his safe. He also learns from her of the association between her and the doctor.

The Chinese doctor establishes an alibi and explains everything in connection with the discovery of the drug and its dispensation by the doctor. Suspicion against the old negro is dropped when he explains to the detective how he saw the doctor's car drive away shortly before the murder was discovered.

After the detective has made numerous efforts to involve the other suspects he concludes that the doctor is the most likely one so he hits on a plan.

Later several persons, who are apparently crazed by a drug, make a raid on the doctor's office and create a panic in his reception room. (Staged by the detectives for psychological effect.) Detectives rush in and tell the doctor that they have learned of his prescribing the virulent drug. They also confront him with what appears to be a confession of the demi-mondaine, implicating the doctor as a murderer. Believing everything to be lost, the doctor confesses.

Then resorting to a ruse of demonstrating to them how he killed the botanist, he suddenly jabs the needle into his own throat and expires.

THE END

This is far from being a complete story plot but it serves to illustrate the method of development from the crude outline and thumbnail synopsis to the more detailed one.

The next step will be to give names to the characters, introduce bits of business and dialogue and write a still more detailed synopsis of several thousand words in length. The characters will now begin to come to life and as the author acquaints himself with them and visualizes their reactions to the various situations in which they find themselves, many bits of action and dialogue will automatically suggest themselves. In the next operation additional or minor characters will also introduce themselves in the proper order and place where the situation demands it. So that when the story is completed by this scientific method of development there will be no unnecessary characters in the story.

An important thing to be remembered here is that by no means does it follow that the continuity of the finished story will be in any way similar to that of the plot synopsis. Developing the plot and telling the story are two separate and distinct things. While the plot synopsis does not disclose the identity of the criminal or guilty person until the very last, the author must of course know who this criminal is and must introduce this person at the very beginning of the story, either as a suspect or otherwise. The manner in which an author opens his story or the angle from which he tackles the problem varies with each and every writer. Thereupon depends his ability to catch the interest of the reader and hold it.

GENERAL INSTRUCTIONS

The Formula and Index of the Detective-Mystery story is of necessity somewhat more complicated than any of the preceding *Genie* series, because of the fact that there must be sub-plots and many angles which give rise to speculation in this type of story.

In order to supply the author with the desired amount of material to provide an interesting plot outline, it has been found necessary to duplicate on some of the nine operations, as will be observed in the following instructions.

The *Plot Genie* tells you *What* happens and when you figure *How* it could happen that way, or when you reconcile the various story elements suggested, one with the other, you will have developed your plot. All of the story elements contained in the Lists and which will appear on the Recording Sheet when one has dialled out a plot outline, are so generalized that plenty of latitude is left for the imagination of the author.

The result of this is that no two authors will develop the same plot from a *Genie* outline. Neither will any two write the same story from a *Genie* plot. This makes it possible for the author to enjoy the advantage of utilizing his knowledge, gained from reading, observation and experience, and to use his creative imagination in any kind of interpretation desired.

DUPLICATION IN LISTS

It might be well to explain that in some of the lists of story elements you will find a certain amount of duplication. The percentage is larger in some lists than others and largest in that of the guilty party. There is a reason for this. This duplication was done for a purpose.

Inasmuch as there are 180 numbers on the Robot disc, it is necessary that each of these lists contain 180 elements in order that no blanks be drawn. We have studiously endeavored to confine these lists to the most novel, colorful, and suggestive material and rather than include that which was undesirable it was thought best to repeat on the other material. Notwithstanding the repetitions it will be found that in dialling for plots the Robot will not, in a thousand times, repeat in the plot outline. Therefore this feature cannot be considered a drawback.

WRITE IN NUMBERS AND ANSWERS FIRST

In order to obtain a plot outline, you should first dial the necessary numbers to fill the appointed spaces on the Recording Sheet. Then you should refer to the Index Lists and write in the answers in the proper spaces. The next step is to write a generalized Thumb-nail synopsis such as the example shown on another page.

You should now study this outline *As A Whole*. Beginning with the first operation and then taking each one in its proper order, you should ask yourself a series of questions as a means of determining *How-When-Where-Who-Why*. When you have satisfactorily arrived at a logical answer for each of these questions you cannot fail to have developed a complete and interesting plot, one that is absolutely original with yourself. Herein lies the secret of the originality of *Genie* plots. No two authors will answer these questions alike.

THE NINE OPERATIONS FOR
THE MURDER MYSTERY

Following are the nine operations which are necessary to dial out a Detective Mystery Story plot outline.

1. Dial once for the victim from List A on page 43, once for the locale from List B on page 47 and once for the tpye of crime from List C on page 51. This tells us who was killed, where and how.

2. Dial once for a clue from List A on page 60 and once for an object under List B on page 69.

3. Dial three times for three suspects from the List on page 73.

4. Inasmuch as there are two lists of methods it is necessary that we first determine which of these is to be used, so we will dial once in order to determine it. If we obtain an even number we use List A on page 77; if an odd number we use List B on page 84. After determining which list to use, then dial once in order to get a number which is to be chosen from the list indicated. The author should now arbitrarily choose one more method from either of these lists—one which does not conflict with the other that has been dialled.

5. There are three lists of Suspicious Circumstances so it is necessary to dial in order to determine which of these lists shall be used. We are going to use three of these elements and obtain them as follows:

   A—Dial a number. Then in order to determine from which list this number shall be chosen, dial again until a number is obtained which ends in a 1-2 or 3.

   B—Dial the second number and then repeat operation above.

   C—Dial the third number and repeat operation above.

6. Dial once for a thrilling situation from the List on page 117.

7. Dial once for a solution from the List on page 124.

8. Dial once for the guilty person from List on page 135.

9. Although we have three lists of motives we can only use one mo-

tive. First, in order to determine which of the lists shall be used, dial until a number is obtained which ends in a 1, 2, or 3. If it ends in 1 use List A, if it ends in 2, use List B, if it ends in 3, use List C. Now dial once more for the number.

If the disc stops so that two numbers are partly showing through the slot, turn it ahead in the direction you have been dialling it to the next number.

This may appear to be a rather complicated set of operations but after it has been practiced for awhile the difficulty will be removed. In order to understand it clearly you should remember that the purpose of the Robot is to arbitrarily supply the author with a series of numbers and answers which comprise an assignment or outline over the formation of which he has had no choice. This is important and necessary if the imagination of the author is to be stimulated into the creation of new and novel plot outlines. If he is permitted merely to pick and choose the various story elements from the lists for his plot, he will automatically and subconsciously select those which have been associated before in other stories and the result will be either a hackneyed plot or an unconscious plagiarism.

When the Robot supplies an outline in which there is an element that is objectionable, it is of course permissible for the author to substitute another element after the brief synopsis has been developed. In many cases he will find in his effort to make this substitution, that the very effort which it is necessary to put forth in order to make the substitution will suggest some new or novel idea or angle.

After all, it reverts to the proposition which we have so many times stated in connection with the use of the *Genie* system of plot building, viz: *Genie* tells you *What* happens and when you figure out *How* it could happen that way you have an absolutely original plot.

OTHER TYPES OF STORIES

You should bear in mind that this *Genie* Formula and Index provides for the writing of Detective-Mystery Stories other than murder mysteries, stories in which the crime may be robbery, destruction of property, kidnapping or forgery.

The nine operations are exactly the same except in the case of Number 1 which determines the nature of the crime committed and in order to secure this information the following directions will suffice.

1. Dial once for a victim to be taken from the List on page 43.
2. The author should himself decide whether the crime shall be robbery, forgery, destruction of property, or kidnapping and should write that in on the Recording Sheet.
3. Dial once for a number and depending upon the last digit in that number will be the element to be used from the proper list. For example, let us suppose that a robbery story is desired and we dial the number 11; we would choose number 1 from List D which appears on page 58 and which tells us that the crime was a robbery of bonds or securities. If we get 115, that would indicate number 5 on the list, which is valuable documents. If 130 appears in the slot in the disc, we would take number 10, which is money; and so on. These instructions will apply to the other three lists as well.
4. Select your own locale after having determined the identity of the victim and the nature of the crime.

OPERATION 1

THE MURDER

Following are three lists which are to be used in connection with the Detective-Mystery murder story. Operation No. 1 in our Formula requires the use of all three of them and tells us who the victim is, where the body was found, and the apparent method that was used to commit the murder.

We should bear in mind then that it is necessary to dial three times or three numbers for this operation. The answer for the first one should be taken from List A, the second from List B, and the third from List C.

Where a repetition appears in any of these lists, it has been done purposely in order to confine the lists to the most colorful material possible, bearing in mind that this Formula and Index is not designed to supply the plot for the so-called "true detective story" but for the scientific and modern detective mystery story.

LIST A

THE VICTIM IS

1. A politician.
2. A countess.
3. A statesman.
4. A college student.
5. A dictator.
6. A modiste.
7. A clown.
8. A ringmaster.
9. An impresario.
10. A motion picture director.
11. A translator.
12. A manikin.
13. A philanthropist.
14. A bon vivant.
15. An archaeologist.
16. A noblewoman.
17. A spiritualist.
18. A trophy hunter.
19. A society belle.
20. A merchant.
21. A captain.
22. A broker.
23. A probation officer.
24. A doctor.
25. A manufacturer.
26. A paramour.
27. A healer.
28. A woman nurse.
29. A juror.
30. A palmist.
31. A foreign emissary.
32. An engineer.
33. A deacon.
34. A governor.

THE VICTIM IS
(Continued)

35. A popular co-ed.
36. A professor.
37. A dramatic critic.
38. An actress.
39. An artist.
40. A gambler.
41. A curio collector.
42. A woman librarian.
43. A princess.
44. A debutante.
45. A ship owner.
46. A reformer.
47. An Egyptologist.
48. A model.
49. A psychologist.
50. A female spy.
51. A prince.
52. A caretaker.
53. A dancer.
54. An inventor.
55. A plastic surgeon.
56. A missionary.
57. A male evangelist.
58. A playwright.
59. A female mystic.
60. A capitalist.
61. A clergyman.
62. A prosecutor.
63. An architect.
64. An hypnotist.
65. A sportsman.
66. A promoter.
67. A public official.
68. A candidate.
69. A scientist.
70. An accountant.
71. A publisher.
72. An underworld queen.
73. A football hero.
74. A female sports star.
75. A nobleman.
76. A demi-mondaine.
77. A college professor.
78. A botanist.
79. An exporter.
80. A lobbyist.
81. An auctioneer.
82. A courier.
83. A famous auto-racer.
84. A judge.
85. A male nurse.
86. A clerk.
87. A hermit.
88. A mystic.
89. A banker.
90. A consul.
91. A radio announcer.
92. A wealthy cattleman.

THE VICTIM IS
(Continued)

93. A bishop.
94. An actor.
95. A psychologist.
96. A statesman.
97. An editor.
98. An auctioneer.
99. An attorney.
100. A monarch.
101. A chemist.
102. A female entertainer.
103. A merchant prince.
104. A governess.
105. A female settlement worker.
106. A bondsman.
107. An autocrat.
108. A woman school teacher.
109. An explorer.
110. An executive.
111. A motion picture actor.
112. A scholar.
113. An antiques collector.
114. A reformer.
115. A professor.
116. A bootlegger.
117. A gem collector.
118. A bibliophile.
119. A chorus girl.
120. A night club dancer.
121. A merchant.
122. A motion picture producer.
123. A popular clubman.
124. A famous polo player.
125. A tennis champion.
126. A woman philanthropist.
127. A novelist.
128. A woman spiritualist.
129. A musician.
130. A woman juror.
131. A judge.
132. A religious worker.
133. A contractor.
134. A prospector.
135. A Secret Service Operative.
136. A mining engineer.
137. A florist.
138. A political exile.
139. A navigator.
140. An assayer.
141. A research chemist.
142. A wealthy recluse.
143. An international spy.
144. A woman artist.
145. A young heiress.
146. A mine owner.
147. A golf champion.
148. A woman probation officer.
149. An animal fancier.
150. A financier.

THE VICTIM IS
(Continued)

151. A woman evangelist.
152. A gigolo.
153. An Oriental.
154. A pawnbroker.
155. A tea merchant.
156. A woman attorney.
157. A hotel keeper.
158. A philanthropist.
159. A woman sculptor.
160. A society leader.
161. A woman judge.
162. A spy.
163. A young millionaire.
164. A photographer.
165. A woman editor.

166. A racketeer.
167. A government official.
168. A Chinese importer.
169. A fur buyer.
170. An English lord.
171. An inventor.
172. An aviation executive.
173. A Bohemian artist.
174. A trader.
175. An administrator.
176. A sculptor.
177. A bacteriologist.
178. A beauty specialist.
179. An interpreter.
180. A cartoonist.

LIST B

LOCALE

THE MURDER IS COMMITTED

1. Aboard ship.
2. In a bank.
3. At a beach club.
4. In the slums.
5. At a ranch house.
6. At a pleasure resort.
7. In a school room.
8. On a mountain side.
9. At a circus.
10. In an office.
11. At an airport.
12. In a casino.
13. Aboard a submarine.
14. At a farmhouse.
15. At a castle.
16. On the docks.
17. At a factory.
18. In a mission.
19. At a mine.
20. In a tavern.
21. In a court room.
22. In a railroad station.
23. At a college.
24. In a caravan.
25. In a theatre.
26. At a shop or store.
27. At a roadhouse.
28. In a boathouse.
29. In a mansion.
30. At a museum.
31. At a hacienda.
32. In Egypt.
33. In a dope den.
34. At a mill.
35. At a dance hall.
36. At a gypsy camp.
37. In a legislative hall.
38. In a dark hallway.
39. In a gymnasium.
40. In an auditorium.
41. On the golf links.
42. At a masque ball.
43. At a tabernacle.
44. In a lighthouse.
45. In the Orient.
46. In a church.
47. In a garden.
48. In an employment office.
49. In a banquet hall.
50. In a hospital.
51. In an oil field.
52. At an observatory.

LOCALE
(Continued)

53. In a haunted house.
54. In a bus.
55. In a hotel.
56. At a motion picture studio.
57. In a subway.
58. In a cabin.
59. On a train.
60. In a newspaper office.
61. On a houseboat.
62. At a radio station.
63. In a vehicle.
64. In a night club.
65. In a dirigible.
66. At an artist's studio.
67. In a financial district.
68. In a cafe.
69. At a deserted village.
70. At a diamond mine.
71. In a salon.
72. At a race track.
73. At a royal court.
74. In a logging camp.
75. At a rectory.
76. At a yacht club.
77. In a taxi.
78. At a speakeasy.
79. At a musical conservatory.
80. At an auto camp.
81. On an Indian reservation.
82. In the Near East.
83. At a spiritualistic hall.
84. At a ranger camp.
85. In a sanitarium.
86. At a carnival.
87. In a laboratory.
88. At a country club.
89. In a deserted house.
90. In a gambling hall.
91. In India.
92. On the docks.
93. In tropical islands.
94. In an airplane.
95. At a ranch house.
96. At a country estate.
97. In a warehouse.
98. In a newspaper office.
99. In a cabaret.
100. In a basement.
101. At a seaside resort.
102. Back stage.
103. In a library.
104. In an office building.
105. In the park.
106. In the forest.
107. In a country club.
108. In a hunting lodge.
109. At a notorious night club.
110. In the patio.

LOCALE
(Continued)

111. In a theatre dressing room.
112. In a penthouse studio.
113. On an ocean liner.
114. In a bunk house.
115. In a radio studio.
116. In a bachelor's apartment.
117. On a wharf.
118. At a music hall.
119. In an underworld dope den.
120. At a smelter.
121. In a haunted inn.
122. In a manor house.
123. In the conservatory.
124. Aboard a submarine.
125. In the vicinity of old ruins.
126. In a coliseum office.
127. On a houseboat.
128. In a secret room.
129. At the race course.
130. In the wine vault.
131. In a factory office.
132. In wings of stage.
133. In a beauty parlor.
134. On a trading schooner.
135. In Senate Chamber.
136. In Sorority or Fraternity house.
137. At a house party.
138. At a banquet.
139. In a museum.
140. At a regatta.
141. In an underground passage.
142. In a doctor's office.
143. In a lady's boudoir.
144. In a depot waiting room.
145. On a ferry boat.
146. On a river steamer.
147. At an old fort.
148. In a billiard room.
149. In the cabin of a yacht.
150. In the subway.
151. On a veranda.
152. At a summer home.
153. In a waterfront speakeasy.
154. At a parsonage.
155. In a temple.
156. In an underground dungeon.
157. In a walled garden.
158. In a border cafe.
159. In a bedroom.
160. In a secret private office.
161. In a hermit's cabin.
162. At a roof garden.
163. In a private car.
164. At a foreign Embassy.
165. In foyer of theatre.
166. In a garage.
167. In a racing stable.

LOCALE
(Continued)

168. In an industrial plant.
169. On a college campus.
170. At the opera.
171. At a chateau.
172. At a trading post.
173. In the Bohemian quarter.
174. At a seance.

175. In an old mission.
176. At a power house.
177. In a Chinese opium den.
178. On a rostrum.
179. In Judge's chambers.
180. In a circus sideshow.

LIST C

THE METHOD OF THE MURDER IS

1. Machine gun fire.
2. A pistol shot in the head.
3. Stabbing with a blunt instrument.
4. Cutting the throat.
5. Drugging, then drowning.
6. Mutilation with a sharp instrument.
7. By an unknown poison.
8. The use of poisoned liquor.
9. Suffocation from contaminated air.
10. Drowning in a body of water.
11. The body is crushed from a fall.
12. Pushing off height.
13. A pistol shot in the body.
14. Stabbing with an arrow.
15. A shot gun wound through the ear.
16. Strangling with cord, wire, or twisted fibre.
17. Mysterious small abrasion under ear.
18. Mysterious administering of a poison.
19. Suffocation by smothering.
20. The body is crushed by a falling object.
21. Burning with acid.
22. The use of a mechanical device.
23. A pistol shot fired into the back.
24. A knife is plunged into the heart.
25. Poisoned with some strange drug.
26. Stabbing with a sword cane.
27. Poison from the bite of a venomous insect.
28. Suffocation from strangulation.

THE METHOD OF THE MURDER IS
(Continued)

29. Burned by fire.
30. A shot gun wound in the head.
31. Being stabbed in the back with a knife.
32. The head is battered in with a blunt instrument.
33. The victim is tortured to death by thirst.
34. Cutting the wrist.
35. Blows resulting from a physical fight.
36. The use of poison in a drug or medicine.
37. Suffocation from choking.
38. A blow on the head from a heavy object.
39. Shot by poisoned arrow.
40. Two small red marks are found on throat.
41. The use of poisoned food.
42. A pistol shot fired into the mouth.
43. Electrocuted by live wire.
44. Choking.
45. A shot gun wound in the body.
46. A small puncture at the base of the brain.
47. Throat cut.
48. Killed by X-ray.
49. The use of poisonous gas.
50. Suffocation is caused by gagging the victim.
51. An anæsthetic is administered.
52. A sword fight.
53. Shot by poisoned dart.
54. A shock of electricity.
55. Starvation.
56. The use of a poisonous needle.
57. Impaling the victim on a sharp spear.

THE METHOD OF THE MURDER IS
(Continued)

58. Mutilation by the bite of an animal.
59. Bruising and crushing the body with a blunt instrument.
60. Smothering with cushions, pillows, draperies, or clothing.
61. The poisonous bite of a venomous reptile.
62. Drowning in a receptacle.
63. The use of a mysterious poison.
64. Burning through the use of electricity.
65. By the explosion of a bomb.
66. A pistol shot in the ear.
67. A deep gash in head.
68. A stab in the heart with a needle or sharp instrument.
69. By blows from a hammer or similar instrument.
70. The use of a blunt instrument to crush the head.
71. A shot gun wound in the back.
72. The use of a poisoned dart or arrow.
73. Suffocation by hanging.
74. The victim is given poisoned water.
75. Killed by discharge of slugs.
76. A shot gun wound in the mouth.
77. The victim is stabbed in the back with a needle.
78. Infection through poisoned disease germs.
79. Suffocation through imprisonment in a hole or small enclosure.
80. Skull crushed by blow.
81. Stabbing with a bayonet.
82. Small puncture on throat.
83. Knife plunged in back.
84. Poisoned bath.
85. Suffocation by garroting.
86. A dagger driven into the heart.

THE METHOD OF THE MURDER IS
(Continued)

87. Decapitation.
88. The opening of an artery.
89. The injection of an air bubble into a blood vessel.
90. With a hand grenade.
91. Neck broken.
92. The body is crushed by an explosion.
93. An anæsthetic is administered.
94. A shock of electricity.
95. Killed by X-ray.
96. A small puncture at the base of the brain.
97. By blow from ax or hatchet.
98. Throat cut by tightly-drawn wire.
99. Skull crushed by blow.
100. Poisoning a drug or medicine.
101. Cutting the wrist.
102. The head is battered in with a blunt instrument.
103. Burning the victim with fire.
104. Poisoning by the use of a venomous insect.
105. A knife is plunged into the heart.
106. The use of a mechanical device.
107. The body is crushed by a falling object.
108. A shot gun wound in the ear.
109. Throat mysteriously lacerated.
110. Drowning the victim in a body of water.
111. Suffocation from contaminated air.
112. The use of poisoned liquor.
113. A pistol shot fired into the mouth.
114. Mutilation with a sharp instrument.
115. The use of poisonous gas.

THE METHOD OF THE MURDER IS
(Continued)

116. Stabbing with a blunt instrument.
117. A shot gun wound in the back.
118. Machine gun fire.
119. Cutting the throat.
120. Bound and tossed into lake, river, or sea.
121. A dagger driven into the heart.
122. A pistol shot in the head.
123. An injection into a blood vessel.
124. The body is crushed by an explosion.
125. A pistol shot in the ear.
126. The victim is given poisoned water.
127. A pistol shot wound in the body.
128. Suffocation by hanging.
129. A scratch from a poisoned thorn.
130. Burning by the use of electricity.
131. The use of a mysterious poison.
132. By ground glass.
133. Bruising and crushing the body with a blunt instrument.
134. Mutilation by the bite of an animal.
135. The poison of a venomous reptile.
136. A shot gun wound in the head.
137. Marks of hypodermic needle on throat.
138. Suffocation by choking.
139. A sword fight.
140. A slender knife plunged into throat.
141. Stabbing with a bayonet.
142. Mysterious administering of a poison.
143. A blow on the head from a sharp object.
144. A misuse of hypnotism.

THE METHOD OF THE MURDER IS
(Continued)

145. By thrust of spear.
146. Starvation.
147. The victim is stabbed in the back with a needle.
148. By a poisoned cosmetic or toilet article.
149. The opening of an artery.
150. By brass knuckles.
151. Stabbing with an arrow.
152. Auto-suggestion or fear.
153. Drowning in a receptacle.
154. Marks of hypodermic needle on throat.
155. Suffocation by smothering.
156. The use of a poisonous needle
157. By a poisoned cosmetic or toilet article.
158. A shot gun wound in the mouth.
159. The injection of an air bubble into a blood vessel.
160. A stab in the heart with a needle or other sharp instrument.
161. Burning with acid.
162. The use of a blunt instrument to crush the head.
163. A pistol shot is fired into the back.
164. By an unknown poison.
165. By rifle shot from a distance.
166. Being stabbed in the back with a knife.
167. Suffocation from strangulation.
168. Infection through poisoned disease germs.
169. Suffocation by garroting.
170. The body is crushed from a fall.
171. A poisoned bath.
172. The victim is tortured to death by thirst.
173. Suffocation through imprisonment in a hole or small enclosure.

THE METHOD OF THE MURDER IS
(Continued)

174. Blows from a physical fight.
175. Slashing the throat.
176. The use of poisoned food.
177. Injection into eye or ear.
178. Decapitation.
179. Suffocation is caused by gagging the victim.
180. By prick of poisoned needle.

LIST D.

ROBBERY

TYPE OF THING TAKEN

1. Bonds or securities.
2. Jewels.
3. Valuable evidence or a clue.
4. A valuable formula or secret instructions.
5. Valuable documents.
6. An object possessing traditional value.
7. An object which has a mystic or occult value.
8. A famous masterpiece.
9. A valuable invention or a scientific discovery.
10. Money.

LIST E.

FORGERY

1. Letter of credit.
2. A document bestowing authority.
3. A deed.
4. A document of evidence.
5. Identification papers.
6. A passport or a release paper.
7. Bonds or securities.
8. A letter of introduction.
9. Valuable legal papers.
10. Checks.

LIST F.

DESTRUCTION OF PROPERTY

1. Dynamiting of property.
2. The setting on fire of property.
3. The destruction of property by explosives.
4. By undermining.
5. By flood or inundation.
6. By chemical means, acids, etc.
7. By the use of lethal gas.
8. By gun fire.
9. By the use of electricity.
10. By an avalanche.

LIST G.

KIDNAPPING OR BABY SNATCHING

1. The kidnapping of a child.
2. The kidnapping of a woman.
3. The kidnapping of an old man.
4. The kidnapping of an old woman.
5. The kidnapping of a dead body.
6. The kidnapping of a servant.
7. The kidnapping of an imbecile.
8. The kidnapping of a guardian.
9. The kidnapping of a leader.
10. The kidnapping of a messenger.

OPERATION 2.

THE OUTSTANDING CLUE IS

The following list provides the author with one or more clues which may be introduced early in the story as pointing to the solution of the crime. These may be used in connection with the murder mystery or any of the other crimes.

In order to complicate the story one may use more than one of these clues if desired but they should be obtained by dialling the Robot and not arbitrarily selected from the list.

It will be observed that following the list of clues is another list of 180 objects, any one or more of which may be found at the scene of the crime and also prove to be a clue, whether false or not.

The author may dial one or more clues from List A and one or more from List B if desired. The purpose is to leave all possible latitude to the story writer in the operation of this formula. Some authors may be satisfied with dialling out a single clue from each list while others will want to complicate matters by introducing a multiplicity of clues.

LIST A.

1. A newspaper clipping, bit of paper or other evidence of an argument.
2. Evidence that the victim has robbed someone.
3. Evidence that the victim has opposed religious freedom.
4. An abrasion or hole in walls, furniture, or earth.
5. Evidence of an old enmity.
6. Evidence that the victim has alienated someone's affection.
7. Evidence of robbery of the victim's person.
8. Persons seen leaving the scene of the crime.
9. Evidence pointing to the height or weight of the criminal.
10. Evidence that the victim had practiced deception.
11. Evidence of the theft of a means of transportation.
12. An assault on a servant of the victim appears to be accidental, but it is discovered by the detective to have been premeditated.
13. The presence of flowers.
14. The existence of an appointment.
15. What appears to be the accidental bombing of a structure is

THE OUTSTANDING CLUE IS
(Continued)

proved by the detective to be the result of a premeditated plan.

16. An incompleted telephone call.
17. A secreted weapon is discovered in a mysterious way.
18. The presence of a book.
19. Evidence reveals the theft of an animal or pet.
20. A mysterious badge or other emblem on the victim's body or at the scene of the crime.
21. The removal of a gem.
22. Evidence that the victim has pursued a reform movement.
23. The erasure or secreting of evidence attempted.
24. The victim is reputed to have recently come into a fortune.
25. Evidence that the victim was a secret and trusted agent.
26. The presence of a photograph.
27. A friend or associate of the victim is assaulted and it is discovered it is deliberate and not accidental.
28. Telegram, cablegram, or radiogram.
29. A mechanism is wrecked apparently accidentally, and the detective discovers it is premeditated action.
30. Presence of the evidence of occultism.
31. A person is secreted and when found will reveal important evidence.
32. Intoxicating liquors.
33. Evidence that the victim was persecuting someone.
34. A hat, garment or other piece of personal apparel is left behind.
35. Evidence that the victim was involved in an international conspiracy.
36. Wherein the victim has been travelling incognito.
37. The presumably accidental assault on a guard is discovered to have been premeditated.

THE OUTSTANDING CLUE IS
(Continued)

38. Method of binding or gagging of victim.
39. Evidence that the victim stood in the way of someone's financial success.
40. An anonymous letter or message.
41. Evidence of the theft of a tool or implement.
42. The presence of a memorandum.
43. A means of escape has been secreted, the discovery of which reveals valuable evidence.
44. Persons seen returning to or hovering about the scene of the crime.
45. Evidence that the victim was involved in an illicit enterprise.
46. Evidence of the theft of a key.
47. The strange brooding of a character.
48. Evidence that the victim had rejected a proposal.
49. The fact that the victim was under an obligation or pledge is revealed.
50. Evidence that the victim anticipated trouble.
51. The presence of a peculiar insect, deposit or bacteria.
52. Evidence that the criminal was wounded.
53. An incompleted letter.
54. Evidence that the victim was spying on someone.
55. The presence of a game of some kind.
56. The discovery of suspicious bills or receipts.
57. The discovery of an exposed negative.
58. The motive of a character is hidden by subterfuge, and when uncovered reveals important evidence.
59. Evidence that the victim was engaged in a fierce rivalry.
60. Hearsay or a rumor.
61. The presence of a statement of accounts.

THE OUTSTANDING CLUE IS
(Continued)

62. Evidence that the victim has balked someone's plans.
63. The destruction of evidence, which appears accidental, is proved by the detective to be the outcome of premeditated action.
64. Evidence that the victim was trying to avoid a person.
65. The presence of blood stains.
66. Evidence that the victim had violated a promise.
67. The presence of a stain other than blood.
68. Evidence that the victim was involved in a faction.
69. Evidence that the victim had a premonition.
70. A peculiar odor left behind.
71. Evidence that the victim has been an obstacle to someone's freedom.
72. A key or other pocket piece left behind.
73. The hiding of an identity creates trouble and reveals an important clue when discovered.
74. Evidence that the victim feared an expose.
75. Evidence that the victim was prosecuting someone.
76. The presence of a mysterious device.
77. Evidence pointing to the Black Hand or other secret organization.
78. Map, plan, or other evidence of premeditated murder or crime.
79. There is a destruction of a means of illumination which appears to be accidental and is proved by the detective to be the result of premeditated action.
80. Evidence of the theft of a book.
81. The victim or some other individual is disguised.
82. Evidence that the victim has a criminal relation.
83. A shred from supposed criminal's apparel.

THE OUTSTANDING CLUE IS
(Continued)

84. Evidence that the victim has prevented a reconciliation.
85. A peculiar pose or position of an object or body.
86. Evidence pointing to revenge.
87. Evidence of the victim's being a fugitive.
88. A bit of handwriting.
89. Evidence that the victim was superstitious.
90. Evidence that the criminal was drunk or drugged.
91. The odd manner in which the victim or some other individual was clothed.
92. Evidence that the victim was trapped.
93. Wherein the victim is impersonating another person.
94. A secret implement or tool is discovered which offers valuable evidence.
95. A transportation ticket.
96. One who resembles the victim is assaulted, presumably by accident, but the detective discovers it was premeditated.
97. The removal of an object.
98. Evidence that the victim was in search of proof.
99. The presence of a mysterious letter or card.
100. Evidence that the victim was involved in a controversy.
101. A facial expression.
102. Evidence that the victim was involved in a political intrigue.
103. Evidence of a struggle.
104. Evidence that the victim was engaged in a private investigation.
105. Foot prints.
106. Evidence that the victim was spied upon.
107. A calling card of the criminal is discovered.
108. Evidence that the victim has been tortured.
109. The discovery of a secret passage.

THE OUTSTANDING CLUE IS
(Continued)

110. Evidence that the victim was engaged in a propaganda campaign.
111. The appearance of strange or colored lights to witnesses.
112. Evidence of the criminal's being a lover of the victim or of a relative of the victim.
113. An automobile or other license number.
114. Evidence of the criminal's being a fugitive.
115. The remainder of a repast or food scraps.
116. Property which has been stolen from the victim and hidden is discovered, revealing important evidence.
117. The contents of a waste basket, grate or other receptacle.
118. Evidence of the robbery of the victim's safe, cabinet or other place of security.
119. Sounds heard by nearby persons.
120. Evidence pointing to a peculiarity of the criminal.
121. A strand or lock of hair, or a wig or toupee.
122. Evidence pointing to the malformity of the criminal.
123. A relative of the victim is assaulted, presumably by accident, but the detective discovers it has been premeditated.
124. Evidence found in dust.
125. The wrecking of a means of transportation is discovered, which proves to be the result of premeditated plans and not of an accident.
126. The discovery of the stealing of identification papers.
127. Evidence that the victim has defrauded someone.
128. A recorded sound.
129. The theft of securities is discovered.
130. A hidden infernal machine is found which offers valuable evidence.

THE OUTSTANDING CLUE IS
(Continued)

131. An incompleted inscription.
132. One who is custodian of evidence is assaulted presumably by accident, but the detective discovers it was premeditated.
133. Evidence that the victim was on one side of a wager.
134. The attempt of the criminal to destroy evidence of the crime— or his connection with it.
135. The stopping of a time piece.
136. Evidence of a bargain having been made.
137. The presence of a chemical or drug.
138. The destruction of a means of communication is discovered which appears accidental until the detective proves it has been deliberately motivated.
139. The presence of an imprint other than finger print or foot print.
140. Evidence that the victim has received threats.
141. The presence of an object which has been dropped.
142 Cigar, cigarette, pipe, or snuff.
143. Voices heard by nearby persons.
144. Evidence of a fight.
145. The presumably accidental assault on a messenger is discovered to have been premeditated.
146. Shadows observed by witnesses.
147. Evidence of forcible entry.
148. A means of escape is destroyed, apparantly through accident, which the detective proves was premeditated.
149. Evidence of the theft of a weapon.
150. Finger prints.
151. A broken object—as evidence of an argument.
152. Hidden valuables are found which offer illuminating evidence.
153. The evidence of the presence of one who is ill or afflicted.

THE OUTSTANDING CLUE IS
(Continued)

154. The discovery of the theft of a document.
155. Evidence that the criminal was disguised.
156. The discovery of a moving picture scene.
157. The presence of an incompleted sketch.
158. Evidence of a hidden means of transportation.
159. A religious aspect is presented.
160. The destruction of defenses which appears to be an accident is proved to be the result of a deliberate move.
161. Footprints of a lower animal or bird.
162. The evidence of superstition on the part of the criminal.
163. The evidence of a peculiar means of escape.
164. A structure is burned apparently accidentally and the detective discovers it was done deliberately.
165. Evidence of scientific knowledge on the part of the criminal.
166. The hiding of a necessary document—discovery of which proves a valuable clue.
167. There is an assault on a loved one of the victim, which is proved to be deliberate, not accidental.
168. Evidence of an idiosyncrasy on the part of the criminal.
169. The presence of a weapon or implement.
170. Evidence of a plot between the victim and the criminal.
171. The imprint of a face on a window pane.
172. Evidence of the use of matches, candle, cigar lighter, flash light or other artificial lighter.
173. The custodian of the victim's valuables is assaulted and events prove the action was premeditated.
174. Evidence of the derangement of the criminal.
175. A peculiar mark on the body of the victim—or at the scene of the crime.

THE OUTSTANDING CLUE IS
(Continued)

176. Evidence that a symbol of authority has been stolen.
177. A means of transportation is burned and investigation reveals it was planned, not accidental.
178. The discovery of an undecipherable message or warning.
179. Evidence that the victim has been involved in a scandal.
180. Evidence that there has been a prophecy of trouble for the victim.

LIST B.

LIST OF OBJECTS

1. A bag or wallet.
2. Any book.
3. Eye glasses.
4. A code.
5. A rocket.
6. A photograph.
7. A badge, medal, decoration.
8. Debris.
9. Electric device.
10. A chain.
11. A bowl.
12. A death mask.
13. A sling.
14. A musical instrument.
15. Scissors.
16. A jewel.
17. Powder.
18. A report.
19. A candle—candlestick.
20. A cartridge—shot.
21. A wire.
22. A button.
23. An amulet.
24. An instrument of a game, as dice, cards, golf clubs.
25. A door knob.
26. A wire.
27. A calendar.
28. An arrowhead or natural souvenir.
29. A bottle of liquor or wine.
30. Any kind of a bomb or parts of one.
31. An emblem, insignia, or coat of arms.
32. A horoscope.
33. A mark.
34. A part of a human body.
35. A court summons.
36. A nail, tacks or brads.
37. A jewel case.
38. Plans.
39. A time detector.
40. A club.
41. A flag, pennant or banner.
42. A gem.
43. An old weapon.
44. A box or case.
45. Binoculars.
46. Spoils or plunder.
47. A lariat or rope or faked rope.
48. Forceps or pliers.
49. A statement or bill.
50. Objects of disguise.
51. A compass.

LIST OF OBJECTS
(Continued)

52. A scrawl on paper or on anything else.
53. A statue or an idol.
54. A lost key.
55. Marked jewelry or other ornament.
56. A walking stick.
57. A driver's license.
58. A bottle of perfume.
59. Weighing scales.
60. An animal.
61. Any kind of shoe.
62. A seal or indication of authority.
63. A stethescope.
64. A plant or flower.
65. A trinket.
66. A household object.
67. An explosive.
68. A plaything.
69. A sketch.
70. A time table.
71. An object of family tradition.
72. Tobacco.
73. Stakes of a wager.
74. An hour glass.
75. A lash.
76. A kodak.
77. A record.
78. An ornament for the house.
79. A surgical instrument.
80. A trademark.
81. A souvenir.
82. A purse or bill folder.
83. An envelope or paper.
84. A holster.
85. A band or bond.
86. Booty or loot.
87. Any kind of pin.
88. A robe or blanket.
89. A preservative.
90. Merchandise.
91. A bit of earth, grass or soil.
92. A hammer or an axe or the handle of one.
93. A utensil.
94. A buckle or clasp.
95. A bulletin.
96. A broken object.
97. A branding iron.
98. A bottle or box of tablets.
99. A binding or bandage.
100. A bone or bones.
101. A bauble.
102. Small safety box or cabinet.
103. A pen or pencil.
104. A leather thong or blackjack.
105. Wearing apparel.

LIST OF OBJECTS
(Continued)

106. A talisman.
107. Brick or clay.
108. A gavel or mallet.
109. A catch or clamp.
110. Fetters or manacles.
111. A grip or valise.
112. A placard.
113. A picture.
114. An object of illumination.
115. Ornaments.
116. Waste or litter.
117. A chart.
118. A caricature.
119. A barometer or other instrument for measuring.
120. A time piece.
121. Cuttings or shavings of wood or metal.
122. Traces of poison.
123. A weapon.
124. A bloodstained cloth.
125. A brush.
126. A disinfectant.
127. A brief case.
128. Any printed matter.
129. A looking glass.
130. A basket or crate.
131. A bottle of medicine.
132. A poem.
133. A hypodermic needle.
134. A half emptied glass or dish.
135. A toilet article.
136. A code.
137. A whistle.
138. A weather glass or vane.
139. Ink writing or mark.
140. A magnet.
141. Makeup stuff.
142. A relic or antique.
143. Loot.
144. Imprint in paraffin or other material.
145. An idol or image.
146. Sculptures.
147. A poisonous animal or insect.
148. A dagger, a dart, or an arrow.
149. A certificate.
150. A hat, cap, or glove.
151. A book mark.
152. A prescription.
153. A rare flower.
154. Some indication of victim's rank.
155. A sensitized object.
156. A time clock.
157. A bird.
158. A thermometer.
159. A drug.

LIST OF OBJECTS
(Continued)

160. A flash light.
161. A fire brand.
162. Any ticket.
163. A painting or sketch.
164. A flask.
165. A glass or dish.
166. A magnifying glass.
167. A pry or lever.
168. A copy of a resignation.
169. Object used in worship.
170. A sliver of certain wood or metal.
171. A whip or crop.
172. Paint or daubs of it.
173. A pinch bar.
174. Gold or other metal.
175. Food or candy.
176. A library card.
177. Marked money.
178. A ruler or tape measure.
179. A search warrant.
180. A paint brush or palette.

OPERATION No 3.

THE PRINCIPAL SUSPECT IS

The following list provides the author with one or more suspects. As in the preceding operation, it is the purpose here to permit the author to dial one or more of these, if desired. As a matter of fact there are in every modern detective-mystery story a number of suspects. There must be in order to keep the reader guessing and to make the story interesting. It is therefore suggested that the author dial several of these suspects, the number depending upon his own desire or method.

It should be borne in mind, of course, that whatever clues have been supplied by the previous operation should be related in some way to the suspects who are provided by this one. Furthermore, it should also be borne in mind that the guilty person who is indicated by Genie must be included among the suspects.

1. A job seeker.
2. An accomplice.
3. A religious maniac.
4. A victim of conspiracy.
5. A colleague.
6. An imitator.
7. Owner of property where crime is committed.
8. A witness.
9. An employee.
10. An invalid.
11. A tyrant.
12. An attempted suicide.
13. A former partner in crime.
14. An experimentor.
15. One who seeks an endowment.
16. One who has confessed to the crime.
17. An immoral woman.
18. A mysterious man.
19. A political agitator.
20. A demented person.
21. A relative.
22. A blackmailer.
23. A prodigy.
24. A feudist.
25. One who is doomed by disease.
26. A fatalist.
27. A cripple.
28. A bootlegger.
29. A supposed coward.
30. One who has been displaced.
31. A friend.
32. An apparition.
33. A business associate.
34. A medium.
35. A craver of excitement.
36. A garrulous person.
37. A doctor.

THE PRINCIPAL SUSPECT
(Continued)

38. A defendant in a suit involving the victim.
39. A practical joker.
40. An agitator.
41. A victim of shell-shock.
42. An alarmist.
43. A reformer.
44. A disguised person.
45. A refugee.
46. One who has been accused by the victim.
47. A partner.
48. The loser of a wager.
49. A defeated antagonist
50. A rival in business.
51. An aspirant for the hand of a female relative.
52. A competitor.
53. The "czar" of a group.
54. The loser in a game.
55. One who fanatically claims to be the criminal.
56. A fortune teller.
57. One who has been deceived.
58. A society girl.
59. A member of an official family.
60. A nurse.
61. A newspaper man.
62. One whose authority is disputed.
63. One who is proved envious of the victim.
64. A critic.
65. An extravagant person.
66. An ex-employer.
67. A caretaker.
68. A sales person.
69. An ex-mate.
70. The discoverer of the crime.
71. A trustee.
72. A customer.
73. A secretary.
74. A body guard.
75. An organizer.
76. A rival for achievement.
77. A hunchback.
78. A wealthy delinquent.
79. A member of a diplomatic family.
80. A favorite.
81. A go-between.
82. A guest.
83. An investigator.
84. An extremist.
85. An hypnotic subject.
86. An ex-partner.

THE PRINCIPAL SUSPECT
(Continued)

87. One whose rights are in dispute.
88. A churchman.
89. A political henchman.
90. A dope or drug peddler.
91. A pagan priest.
92. An accuser.
93. A rival in love.
94. A messenger.
95. An exile.
96. A stickler for a tradition.
97. A Chinese.
98. A sportsman.
99. A tramp.
100. A dive keeper.
101. Another person's husband or wife.
102. A curio hunter.
103. A gangster.
104. One who claims to be the criminal.
105. A spy.
106. A foreigner.
107. A gypsy.
108. A mysterious woman.
109. One who is suspected of conspiracy.
110. An ex-convict.
111. The loser of a loved one.
112. A half-wit.
113. One who has been rebuked.
114. An idealist.
115. A sub-contractor.
116. A Japanese servant.
117. A passerby.
118. A victim of conspiracy.
119. A rival in business.
120. A circus barker.
121. A beach comber.
122. A river rat.
123. A pseudo-nobleman.
124. A mystic.
125. A fiend.
126. A fugitive.
127. An animal.
128. An ex-servant.
129. An aspirant for the hand of a male relative.
130. An heir or an heiress.
131. An Oriental.
132. A Hindu.
133. A racketeer.
134. An adventurer.
135. One who has confessed to a crime.
136. An Apache.
137. A peon.
138. A communist.

THE PRINCIPAL SUSPECT
(Continued)

139. A voyageur.
140. A promoter.
141. A counterfeiter.
142. A forger.
143. A neurotic.
144. A protege.
145. A delivery man.
146. An ex-employee.
147. An entertainer.
148. A bookmaker.
149. A dancing partner.
150. A ward boss.
151. A voodoo doctor.
152. An East Indian.
153. An Octoroon servant.
154. A night club owner.
155. A gem collector.
156. A fisherman.
157. A step-brother or sister.
158. The loser of a loved one.
159. One who is suspected of conspiracy.
160. A step-father or mother.

161. An ape-man.
162. A lover of wife or beloved of husband.
163. A half-breed.
164. A man with wooden leg.
165. A one-eyed man.
166. A millionaire clubman.
167. A family lawyer.
168. A cousin.
169. A business adviser.
170. An escaped convict.
171. An electrician.
172. An itinerant peddler.
173. An heir-presumptive.
174. A district attorney.
175. An explorer.
176. A housekeeper.
177. A disappointed suitor, sweetheart or lover.
178. An antiques collector.
179. An anarchist.
180. A ward.

OPERATION No. 4

THE METHOD OF INVESTIGATION EMPLOYED BY THE INVESTIGATOR TO SOLVE THE PROBLEM IS

The method of detecting a crime or solving a mystery varies with investigators or detectives. The two lists which follow supply the author with concrete suggestions as to how he shall have his detective proceed. Not only do these suggestions have that value but it will be found that when they are combined with the preceding and following elements, new and interesting trains of thought will invariably be set in motion, resulting in novel ideas.

There being two lists it is, of course, necessary for the author to determine which one to use, as described in the General Directions in the front of the book. If desired as a means of providing a more complete plot outline, the author may dial the Robot for one of these elements and then select one or more others which logically adapt themselves to it.

LIST A

1. There is an investigation of relatives.
2. Reference is made to a blue book.
3. An old affiliation is traced.
4. A warrant is issued.
5. A bold adventure is undertaken.
6. A curio shop is investigated.
7. A woman in the case is sought.
8. A blunder is purposely made.
9. A confederate is sought.
10. A stimulant is administered.
11. Tracing of dental work is employed.
12. Plans are suddenly abandoned.
13. An intoxicating drug or liquor is used.
14. There is ostensibly an accession.
15. The use of a dummy or decoy detective is made.
16. Shadowing
17. The tracing of an animal.
18. Resort to a long wait in order to cow suspect.
19. A possession is suddenly acquired.

THE METHOD EMPLOYED
(Continued)

20. A flame or fire is used.
21. The past of a character is investigated.
22. There is a bombardment.
23. There is a minute inspection of personal properties.
24. A child is used as a decoy.
25. There is an adulteration of material, matter, or liquid.
26. A comedy is staged.
27. A dictaphone is utilized.
28. Employment is given.
29. A fanatic is placed under observation.
30. A mysterious infection is investigated.
31. A strange weapon is employed, sought or investigated.
32. Clever action is employed.
33. An incessant noise or action is utilized for effect.
34. The payment of money is stopped.
35. A character is kidnapped.
36. A strange or peculiar creed is investigated.
37. A melodrama is staged.
38. Temporary paralysis is caused.
39. A strange prayer is made.
40. The whereabouts of a person is investigated.
41. A sudden and unexpected accusation is made.
42. Announcement that investigation has been dropped is made to throw criminals off guard.
43. Tracing of laundry marks is made.
44. Reconstruction of shattered or disintegrated object or body is attempted.
45. An old adage is employed.
46. A position is wiped out.
47. An inanimate object is vivified.

THE METHOD EMPLOYED
(Continued)

48. A mysterious breakdown is planned.
49. A cache is sought.
50. A character is blindfolded.
51. A daredevil stunt is planned.
52. A prisoner is apparently given his freedom and his movements are watched.
53. A suspect is lead to believe that another suspect has confessed.
54. An absorbent is employed.
55. A theory of fatalism is investigated.
56. It is planned to produce an illusion.
57. A character is presumably killed.
58. Research is made in a library.
59. A morbid tendency is investigated.
60. A strange vehicle is employed.
61. Ventriloquism is used.
62. Attempt is made to trace origin of tattoo marks.
63. Investigation is made of threats.
64. A signal which is expected by suspect is counterfeited.
65. There is an abduction.
66. A gangster is put under observation or questioned.
67. An hereditary tendency is studied.
68. A gross exaggeration is employed.
69. A concealed kodak is used.
70. Machine guns or other terrible weapons are set up.
71. A clever illustration is produced for effect.
72. An apparent miracle is staged or investigated.
73. Appeal is made to a prejudice.
74. An old adversary is introduced.
75. A ghastly impression is made.
76. A brothel is searched.

THE METHOD EMPLOYED
(Continued)

77. A camouflage is arranged or penetrated.
78. An unknown lover or sweetheart is sought.
79. Attempt is made to break down a morale.
80. Reflection by mirrors or otherwise is employed.
81. A concealed vault is sought.
82. A license number is traced.
83. Use is made of mental torture.
84. The suspect is provided with an alibi.
85. A loved one of the suspect is placed in great jeopardy.
86. A venomous reptile or vicious animal is employed.
87. Bacillus is used or traced.
88. A newspaper article is published.
89. Brutality is employed.
90. An apparent concession is made.
91. The process of deduction is employed.
92. It is planned to cause an exhaust of strength.
93. Suspect is surrounded with a number of disguised people.
94. An abnormal person or thing is employed.
95. Action involving a graveyard is planned.
96. A harlot is placed under observation.
97. The presence of an insect is investigated.
98. The connection of a Hindu is investigated.
99. A fake lynching is staged.
100. An apparent mystery is introduced for effect.
101. A rapid advance is made.
102. The use of fright is employed.
103. A startling announcement is made.
104. An illicit love is investigated.
105. The use of kindness is employed for effect.

THE METHOD EMPLOYED
(Continued)

106. A loathsome object is introduced.
107. Publicity is threatened or employed.
108. Suspect is threatened with proof of a greater crime which he has committed.
109. Suspect is placed in the position of being obliged to sacrifice an innocent.
110. An addict is employed.
111. An extradition is proposed.
112. A beacon is erected.
113. A motion picture camera is employed.
114. A body is exhumed.
115. A department or departure is abolished.
116. There is the flushing of a receptacle or conduit in search of evidence.
117. A bribe or premium is offered.
118. Burglary is committed or planned.
119. A fake accident is staged.
120. A strange instrument is brought into play.
121. The suspect is permitted to carry out further criminal plans in order to catch him in the act.
122. Advantages are taken of an affection.
123. A hideous sight is planned for effect.
124. An incision is made in search of evidence.
125. An unexpected aggressor is made to play a part.
126. A dummy postmark or other mark of identification is prepared to mislead the criminal.
127. A facsimile of an object in evidence is utilized.
128. There is a clever disguise used.
129. An affinity is traced.

THE METHOD EMPLOYED
(Continued)

130. A novel method is utilized in giving a signal.
131. Frivolous behavior is investigated.
132. An unexpected affront is employed.
133. A large body of liquid is drained.
134. A fake fight is staged.
135. The worship of a pagan god is investigated.
136. There is a lookout for effect.
137. An interpreter is employed.
138. Martial law is threatened or declared.
139. A puzzle or enigma is propounded.
140. An affliction is investigated.
141. A relationship is annulled.
142. A doctor is called in.
143. An old grievance is probed.
144. A laboratory is used.
145. Aggravation is employed.
146. A deformity is simulated.
147. An ancestor is investigated.
148. Blackmail is threatened.
149. Dice or instruments of gambling are employed.
150. A professional impersonator is sought.
151. The services of an alienist are employed.
152. An anonymous communication is sent.
153. An explosion or shot is imitated for effect.
154. A gamble or wager is investigated.
155. Amnesia is simulated.
156. The connection of a lawyer is probed.
157. The use of magnets or magnetism is employed. (Science fiction.)
158. A talisman is produced, searched or investigated.

THE METHOD EMPLOYED
(Continued)

159. Modern science is employed.
160. An unexplained altercation is caused to take place.
161. An insinuating annoyance is employed.
162. The use of a crucifix is made.
163. An old album is sought.
164. An article is apparently lost or mislaid in the way of the suspect.
165. A brotherhood is investigated.
166. Incense is burned for effect.
167. A significant event of history is scrutinized.
168. An exciting agitation is begun.
169. A clever hoax is staged.
170. An insolvency is probed.
171. Advantage is taken of an illness.
172. A chemical reaction is employed.
173. A person feigns to be asleep.
174. The use of boasting is employed.
175. A clandestine meeting is spied upon.
176. An underworld connection is investigated.
177. A rapid transformation is employed.
178. There is a strange alteration made.
179. Bloodhounds are used.
180. An apparently crazy person is employed.

OPERATION No. 4

THE METHOD OF INVESTIGATION EMPLOYED BY THE INVESTIGATOR TO SOLVE THE PROBLEM IS—

LIST B

1. The use of an amateur investigator is employed.
2. A character apparently runs amuck.
3. A sudden and unexpected attack is launched.
4. A barricade is erected.
5. There is a clever delusion used.
6. An object is duplicated.
7. An obstacle is erected.
8. A powerful man or woman is forced to abdicate.
9. An old feud is investigated.
10 An appeal is made to the appetite.
11 A bucolic announcement is made.
12. An autopsy is performed.
13. A betrayal is planned.
14. A conduit or connection is sought.
15. Sudden and terrible anxiety is simulated.
16. A family history is traced.
17. An illicit traffic is probed.
18. An imperfection is scrutinized.
19. A lethal gas is sought or employed.
20. A marriage is investigated.
21. The affections of a person are purposely alienated.
22. There is an ambush.
23. A cripple is employed.
24. A mournful dirge is contrived.
25. A sensational expose is planned.
26. A secret analysis is made.

THE METHOD EMPLOYED
(Continued)

27. A significant anecdote is related.
28. A corpse is used.
29. A deaf mute is simulated or employed.
30. An heritage is investigated.
31. An injunction is sought.
32. A supposed interstellar visitor is sought or investigated. (Science fiction.)
33. A labyrinth is employed for effect.
34. The crime of arson is simulated.
35. An eerie scene is staged.
36. A flirtation is contrived or investigated.
37. Agonizing pain is caused.
38. A strange ritual is sought or employed.
39. A strange and unusual penalty is threatened or inflicted.
40. A fake sacrifice is made.
41. Attempt is made to trace tracks or imprints.
42. It is planned to catch the suspect unawares or when his defense is greatly weakened.
43. An arrest is made for effect.
44. A capture is attempted.
45. A fake confession is made.
46. An apparition is employed.
47. A blind person is employed or simulated.
48. The science of mathematics is employed to confuse.
49. An impressive array is displayed.
50. An effort is made to bewilder.
51. A heated fake argument is staged.
52. An armistice is declared.
53. A dispute is precipitated.

THE METHOD EMPLOYED
(Continued)

54. An imbecile, either real or supposed, is placed under observation.
55. An apparatus is employed.
56. A deformity is counterfeited.
57. An apparent paradox is produced for effect.
58. Anxiety and suspense are employed.
59. An appeal is made to conscience.
60. A pathetic scene is staged or described for effect.
61. A sacred object is sought, produced, or withheld.
62. Somnambulism is investigated.
63. A venomous reptile or insect is sought or employed.
64. A strange sacrifice is probed.
65. Torture is employed.
66. A fainting spell or spells are feigned.
67. An aroma is employed or investigated.
68. Advantage is taken of a tryst.
69. An attempt is made to trace labels, serial numbers, or manufacturer's marks.
70. Microscopic analysis is made of hair, nails, thread, ash, or other minute clues.
71. An artificial limb is employed.
72. The use of bluff is employed.
73. A situation of chaos is perpetrated.
74. An artificial object is used.
75. There is a confiscation of property.
76. A scene or situation is dramatized.
77. An asylum is investigated.
78. The use of the Bible is employed.
79. A pagan performance is staged for effect.
80. A cataclysm is threatened.

THE METHOD EMPLOYED
(Continued)

81. A derelict is introduced.
82. A fiendish motive is sought.
83. A prophesy is studied for evidence.
84. A peculiar 'ideal is investigated.
85. A caricature is made.
86. Electricity is employed.
87. A colony is invaded.
88. A liberty is restrained.
89. A strange intoxicant is investigated.
90. A challenge is offered.
91. A habit is studied.
92. A trial is faked.
93. Persuasive argument is used.
94. A sudden change is indicated.
95. A drunkard is simulated.
96. Facial characters are altered or investigated.
97. Clairvoyance is used.
98. An excavation is made.
99. The use of invisibility is plotted. (Science fiction.)
100. An international complication is probed.
101. The operation of a peculiar law is studied.
102. An important comparison is studied.
103. Flattery is adopted for effect.
104. It is planned to make an invasion.
105. Lavish expenditure is investigated.
106. A clan is investigated.
107. A collision is staged.
108. A subtle demonstration is employed.
109. A dwarf is employed.
110. A forcible entry is made.

THE METHOD EMPLOYED
(Continued)

111. An exciting escape is simulated.
112. A homicidal tendency is investigated.
113. An iron clad armor is used.
114. Evidence of the presence of a maniac is traced.
115. The use or effect of hypnosis is investigated.
116. An itinerant person is sought.
117. Mimicry is employed.
118. An operation is threatened or performed.
119. A fake panic is staged.
120. A hobby is investigated.
121. An imperial association is sought.
122. A mental reaction is studied.
123. A mistress is sought.
124. A person's hysterical behavior is probed.
125. A strange manifesto is investigated.
126. Patience is purposely exhausted.
127. An old opponent is introduced or investigated.
128. A spiritualistic medium is employed.
129. An embarrassing questionnaire is used.
130. A character is reduced to pauperism.
131. A mob is utilized for effect.
132. A significant measurement is made.
133. A strange phenomenon is produced for effect.
134. There is a masquerade employed.
135. A posthumous creation is investigated.
136. A proxy is employed.
137. The suspect is placed in the position of being obliged to sacrifice a friend or loved one.
138. A manikin is employed.
139. A surprising prank is employed.

THE METHOD EMPLOYED
(Continued.)

140. An exotic perfume is investigated.
141. A monotonous sound or movement is employed for effect.
142. A mystic or magician is employed.
143. A strange penance is investigated.
144. An old proverb is scrutinized for connection.
145. A chimera is encouraged.
146. An appeal is made to conceit.
147. A midget is employed or investigated.
148. A counterfeit copy is sought.
149. A monstrosity is produced.
150. A convict is sought.
151. An entertainment is staged.
152. An eviction is made.
153. The cause of a persecution is probed.
154. A bold dash is made.
155. An enigma is offered.
156. An examination is made of hotel registers.
157. The apparent presence of a dead person is contrived.
158. A play is made upon the cupidity of suspect's confederate.
159. Use is made of radio.
160. There is a cross- examination of the family and friends of the victim.
161. Psycho-analysis is employed.
162. A person whom investigator knows is innocent is arrested for effect.
163. There is intimidation of loved one of suspect.
164. The third degree is used.
165. The services of a handwriting expert are employed.
166. Brain tissue is subjected to chemical analysis.
167. Investigator resorts to bargaining with suspect.

THE METHOD EMPLOYED
(Continued)

168. Use is made of lip reading.
169. The family and friends of suspect are subjected to cross-examination.
170. There is a reconstruction of the crime for effect.
171. The psychological method of word-association is used.
172. There is a play upon the superstition of the suspect.
173. Investigator impersonates a criminal to secure information.
174. Intimidation of suspect is resorted to.
175. Cross-examination of suspect is employed.
176. Television is used.
177. Investigator resorts to bargaining with suspect's confederate.
178. Recourse is had to the process of elimination.
179. The services of a blood analyst are employed.
180. A play is made upon the fear of the suspect.

OPERATION No. 5.

A SUSPICIOUS CIRCUMSTANCE OR BAFFLING SITUATION IS

In every interesting detective-mystery story there must be one or more suspicious circumstances which not only baffle the detective or investigator in the story but also cause speculation on the part of the reader. The three lists following provide such material. Any one of these may prove to be either a real clue or a false scent which temporarily throws the investigator off the track. The author may use one or more of these as desired, but they should be obtained from the list by dialling the Robot and not by arbitrary selection. The method of determining which of the three lists to use is described in the General Directions in the front of the book.

LIST A.

1. A campaign or an action or plan abandoned at the same time the crime is committed.
2. A peculiar entrance to a room or other compartment.
3. A mysterious message is discovered on a dictaphone or phonograph record.
4. An attempt to conceal information concerning business affairs.
5. A person is found to be guilty of a minor offense which seems to have a bearing on the case.
6. A scientific discovery proves or disproves some theory or evidence.
7. On or about the time the crime is committed, a mysterious fire or blaze is observed.
8. Some person is seen boarding a ship, train, plane, bus, hurriedly or surreptitiously.
9. Sculpture or other art work discovered to have some bearing on the case.
10. When consternation results from the display of a search warrant.
11. The abrupt termination of an interview when a mention of the crime is made.
12. The unexplained absence of some person.

A SUSPICIOUS CIRCUMSTANCE
(Continued)

13. The concealment of a cablegram, telegram, or radiogram is uncovered.
14. A person or body or animal is found caged in any kind of compartment, box or enclosure.
15. A person has received a mysterious call.
16. It is discovered that a person has slandered or cast aspersions upon another.
17. A person demands a writ of habeas corpus.
18. An important object or piece of furniture is mutilated.
19. The incoherent talk of a half-wit.
20. A suspicious separation of persons or dissolution of partnership or association involved.
21. An attempt to shanghai a person.
22. A person is shocked at certain insinuations or information.
23. The use of some delicate apparatus is found near scene of crime.
24. The discovery of a clever camouflage.
25. A secret settlement of division of property.
26. A person fakes hallucination.
27. A call for help has been answered or denied.
28. An unexplained cash transaction concealed or revealed.
29. The discovery of a part of a body.
30. A clock or time piece has been tampered with.
31. A collection of valuables has been broken into or separated.
32. A sudden departure from a conference.
33. The disappearance of a person.
34. Admittance to a place is denied.
35. A person has remarked that the victim deserved hanging, or other type of killing.
36. A discovery that a person is brokenhearted over love or trouble.
37. Some one is found wearing a steel vest.

A SUSPICIOUS CIRCUMSTANCE
(Continued)

38. An old legend is described as having a bearing on the case.
39. A card, letter or other form of communication which has been concealed, is discovered.
40. The deportment of a character—acting absent-minded or pretending absentmindedness.
41. The unexpected abuse of a person which would arouse suspicion.
42. The discovery that an entrance is made difficult by the presence of a gas.
43. Effort to smuggle something out of state or country.
44. Discovery that there is a stigma against one's name.
45. The check-up of the time of a storm, or its effects.
46. An attempt at suicide is prevented.
47. Discovery that a person hates another, or the victim, and has made such a statement.
48. A conflict is discovered to have taken place over a game, race or event.
49. A peculiar accident to some person.
50. Giving out the wrong address.
51. A mysterious advertisement.
52. A person's authority is questioned.
53. A mechanical device is used for an alibi.
54. The registering of a certain instrument disproves some important evidence.
55. A person is discovered to be or have been a henchman of victim or other important character.
56. Discovery of a cache of money—a weapon— a part of a body— of clothes.
57. The strange or mysterious action of a person.

A SUSPICIOUS CIRCUMSTANCE
(Continued)

58. Publication of wrong information and the discovery that it is false.
59. A person changes place with an inanimate object or vice versa.
60. The overhearing of a speech formula.
61. The manner in which the discoverer of the crime gave the alarm.
62. The unusually haggard or worried appearance of some person.
63. An agreement is secretly cancelled.
64. A supposed amateur is discovered to be a professional in his line
65. A person who claimed to be alone is discovered to have had a companion.
66. Concealment of the receipt of an allotment or an allowance.
67. The unexpected abuse of an animal arousing suspicion.
68. Concealing an effort to clean up debris.
69. Knowledge of an alarm is withheld.
70. There is a defamation of character suit threatened.
71. The unexpected discovery of an unusual character.
72. A discrepancy discovered in a person's recital of an event in connection with the crime.
73. Suspicion is thrown upon one who has employed investigator.
74. The playing of a significant tune or melody.
75. An attempt to carry an object from one place to another rouses suspicion.
76. The concealed plans for a celebration are uncovered.
77. The use of some unusual means of transportation by some person.
78. The sudden mysterious illness of some person.
79. The unexplained concealment of an important certificate.
80. A person loses his composure in an interview or on being accosted.

A SUSPICIOUS CIRCUMSTANCE
(Continued)

81. The discovery that a supposedly dead person is alive.
82. An attempt to humiliate a person.
83. A supposed imbecile reveals concealed object or secreted evidence.
84. The presence of a poisonous reptile or insect.
85. Unexpected political affiliations discovered — legitimate or otherwise.
86. A refusal to admit an identity.
87. The discovery that suicide has been attempted and the fact concealed.
88. Mysterious, but apparently unnecessary, concealing of article of clothing.
89. Discovery that a person is an imposter.
90. A person attempts to retract an accusation.
91. A person is discovered tied and bound or gagged.
92. A time detector or regulator is discovered.
93. An attempt to conceal apparel.
94. It is revealed that a person has been influenced by a horoscope.
95. A person denies a humane act to victim or other person in trouble.
96. A person is discovered in an effort to conceal facts.
97. An unusual person is discovered to be the admirer of the victim.
98. Coffee, tea, or other drink has been contaminated or poisoned.
99. The discovery of an unexplained power to fascinate causes a person to become suspected.
100. A co-worker refuses to carry on a project.
101. A suspect brags over the detective's inability to discover his connection with the crime.
102. A door, panel, box or what not has been mysteriously closed.
103. A person is discovered in a comatose state.

A SUSPICIOUS CIRCUMSTANCE
(Continued)

104. An attempt to make or offer a compromise.
105. Supposedly valuable jewels or other things discovered to be faked.
106. Provisions of a will, heretofore generally concealed.
107. Saving of a life interfered with.
108. It is discovered that the use of some form of magic has been made.
109. The double meaning of an anecdote rouses suspicion.
110. A chemical analysis produces unexpected results.
111. A person is given or gives wrong directions as to a location.
112. It is revealed that evidence of a struggle has been concealed.
113. Discovery that a person has frequented a questionable place.
114. A check-up in the matter of time discloses a discrepancy.
115. A person is discovered to have an hereditary peculiarity.
116. A humorous accusation or statement proves to be serious.
117. Report is received of a clandestine meeting.
118. An unexpected claimant to valuables appears.
119. A place has been unexpectedly cleaned up.
120. The use of drugs has been concealed.
121. A suspicious effort to compensate a suspect or other person.
122. A person has been or is discovered in a compromising position.
123. Discovery that treasure, valuables or other things have been hoarded.
124. A suspected person attempts to conceal a hurt or a wound, or destroy evidence of how it was done.
125. Concealing of illicit selling or trading.
126. An attempt to implicate one hitherto unsuspected.
127. A person suddenly changes his mind.
128. The discovery of a strange alliance between persons.

A SUSPICIOUS CIRCUMSTANCE
(Continued)

129. Unexpected agony of a person revealing a hitherto unsuspected wound.
130. Secret invention concealed and effort made to find it.
131. Intimacy between unusual types of people.
132. Actions that point to insanity.
133. Discovery regarding a person's insurance.
134. A drink is discovered to contain liquor or poison.
135. A person attempts to conceal his dash for freedom when caught.
136. The discovery that some person is concealing facts.
137. The discovery that a supposedly absent person is present.
138. Concealing or destroying things involved in an inheritance.
139. The discovery of suspicious tracks.
140. The manner or action of a person is incongruous or not in keeping with his known character.
141. A noise or sound is counterfeited or imitated.
142. The discovery that some character had a key in his possession.
143. A person changes his first story about the crime, or anything even remotely involving it.
144. The discovery that some person is using an alibi.
145. The destruction of a means of alarm is discovered.
146. Attempt to conceal evidence of an altercation.
147. It is discovered that a person has secretly put a curse or anathema on the victim.
148. A letter or published statement has a double meaning.
149. The discovery of a concealed animal.
150. Concealing an attempt to punish a person.
151. The discovery of a strange mechanism.
152. A person attempts to conceal sorrow.
153. The unexpected discovery of human remains.
154. Discovery that an anaesthetic has been used.

A SUSPICIOUS CIRCUMSTANCE
(Continued)

155. A lawful right is denied some one secretly.
156. Flickering or turning out of light at a certain time.
157. A peculiar device attached to a lock is discovered.
158. The discovery that tracks have been obliterated.
159. Effort to conceal a purchase.
160. The discovery that a postmark or other mark of identification has been forged.
161. A bed not slept in.
162. It is discovered that an imaginary character who has been created mysteriously disappears.
163. The discovery that the features of a character had been altered.
164. A person thought to be superior proves himself otherwise.
165. A person's superstitious fear discovered.
166. A failure in the delivery of a message.
167. Revelation that one person has terrorized another.
168. An attempt has been made to throw away some object which supposedly has some bearing on the case.
169. The time of the crime has been variously reported or concealed and is discovered.
170. Discovery that some one has taken unusual precautionary measures.
171. The discovery that a door or gate had been opened.
172. A person takes the blame to prevent another's being involved in the case.
173. Where a person appears to be faking insanity.
174. A mechanical device conceals the absence of a person.
175. Evidence of a threat to kill has been concealed and is uncovered.
176. A person becomes confused in the story he is telling.
177. A connoisseur pretends ignorance of his subject.
178. The credentials of an important character are stolen.

A SUSPICIOUS CIRCUMSTANCE
(Continued)

179. The discovery that an imitation or substitute set-up of some kind has been made.
180. Patronage of a wealthy or authoritative person is suddenly and secretly withdrawn.

OPERATION No. 5.

A SUSPICIOUS CIRCUMSTANCE OR BAFFLING SITUATION IS—

LIST B.

1. The attempt to destroy evidence of antagonism between victim and a person.
2. An apparently insignificant action—such as telephoning, sending a message, etc.—becomes important when it is discovered that it occurred near the time of the crime.
3. A mechanical device creates the appearance through sound, shadow, etc., of a human being.
4. An attempt is made to conceal a label or other indication of the purchase of an object sought or used in evidence.
5. A person pretends friendship with one he had never seen before.
6. A person in a trance makes surprising announcements.
7. An effort to spread contagion.
8. The overhearing of a conversation of a suspect, in which he refutes his story.
9. Unexplained attempt at communication.
10. A person's credentials proved false.
11. The plot of further crime discovered.
12. A person attempts to conceal the fact that he has been crippled.
13. The discovery of concealed evidence of a crime.
14. A person is deprived of rank or degree.
15. A magnet is discovered which has been used for some unusual purpose.
16. Concealment of a person whose liberty stirs up trouble.
17. A person who feigns friendship is discovered to be jealous of another.

A SUSPICIOUS CIRCUMSTANCE
(Continued)

18. A concealed marked calendar or other reference to a date or an hour.
19. A person becomes confused when he is confronted with suspected evidence.
20. The evasion of the terms of a contract.
21. The discovery that a character has been brooding.
22. A strange request for information.
23. Intimate knowledge of victim's habits and peculiarities apparently known to suspect.
24. Unusual animosity displayed by pet of victim for suspect.
25. Similar cabalistic tattoo or other marks of identification on both victim and suspect.
26. The discovery of the existence of a strange relationship.
27. A person who has pretended lack of knowledge is discovered to be suspiciously familiar with details.
28. Repeated use of cryptic remarks.
29. The discovery of an abandoned vehicle.
30. The defalcation of funds has been concealed.
31. A person is found to be mentally deficient or delinquent.
32. Curiosity causes a person to forget caution.
33. The cruelty of a character arouses suspicion.
34. Money dedicated to a certain purpose arouses antagonism.
35. A person supposedly just returned from a tour, discovered to have been back for a length of time.
36. The attempt to destroy or conceal an animal.
37. The discovery of the concealment of evidence of antagonism.
38. A person deliberately jeopardizes a position or condition of safety.
39. An attempt to conceal jewels, money, or other valuables.

A SUSPICIOUS CIRCUMSTANCE
(Continued)

40. Discovery that a person claims no acquaintance with one whom he knows.
41. A supposed decoration is discovered to be used for concealing something of importance.
42. An underworld character is discovered to be interested in the case.
43. An effort to correspond with another seceretly.
44. A person caught in an embarrassing situation gives contradictory explanation.
45. A reservation for secret and rapid transportation is found.
46. A secret meeting of persons arouses suspicion.
47. Something is discovered which appears to have been saturated with poison or anaesthetic.
48. Discovery of a death mask which has been concealed.
49. An erratic declaration on the part of some person.
50. The apparently accidental discharge of a weapon.
51. A good spender ceases to spend freely.
52. The presence of a maniac.
53. A secret marriage is discovered.
54. A person unexpectedly shows undue anxiety.
55. Discovery that a person is faking aphasia.
56. A person is discovered to be evading the law.
57. An effort is made to mislead investigator with a false clue.
58. A legatee is unexpectedly produced or discovered.
59. An effort to conceal correspondence of victim or some other important character.
60. The discovery that some one is being shadowed or trailed.
61. The discovery that disaster has been foretold by fortune teller.
62. Garrulity of a drug addict.
63. Sudden change in plans of victim known to suspect.

A SUSPICIOUS CIRCUMSTANCE
(Continued)

64. A crytical utterance is overheard.
65. The discovery that some one has unexpectedly paid up all his bills preparatory to a move.
66. Secret attempt to placate or appease a person.
67. The unexpected appearance of a missing person.
68. An attempt to conceal an argument or the fact that there has been one.
69. The presence of a baffling odor, aroma or perfume.
70. Discovery of correspondence or other personal writing, such as diary.
71. A guide deliberately misleads his party.
72. An attempt on the part of some person to use a decoy.
73. Discovery that a person has used a vehicle and concealed the fact.
74. An unusual person believed innocent, offers himself into custody.
75. The decrease of the victim's or another important person's income.
76. The defacement or distortion of an object or thing.
77. Discovery of an effort to delete words, signs, or phrases from any communication.
78. The victim or another person has a guard, for safety or otherwise.
79. Discovery of a secret love affair.
80. Location of a looking glass and what it could reflect.
81. Discovery that a person is faking amnesia.
82. The discovery that a person has made a strange appeal.
83. Concealment of the fact that a person has received help or a threat.

A SUSPICIOUS CIRCUMSTANCE
(Continued)

84. Discovery that an apparently valueless trinket is not what it seems.
85. A peculiar machine which has been concealed is discovered.
86. Unexpected or unexplained malicious action of a person.
87. Discovery of an artificial covering of verdigris, sod, or other covering.
88. A person attempts to conceal an effort to default.
89. The secret attempt to defend a person under suspicion.
90. Hidden writing brought to light by chemical, erasures, etc.
91. A visa or other official document of identification is discovered.
92. It is revealed that a character has attacked the name of another unmercifully.
93. Concealed threat against a person's life—victim or otherwise.
94. The love of a person for the victim or another—warranted or otherwise.
95. A person is discovered to be on a leave of absence.
96. The victim or another has been threatened with a lawsuit.
97. An attempt to defraud the victim or another important person.
98. Discovery that self-possession, self-assurance, or self-confidence is forced, unreal.
99. The destruction of evidence of an appointment.
100. A person is discovered to be involved with one of questionable character.
101. The discovery that a safety device or precautionary measure has been removed or altered.
102. Babblings of a weak-minded person.
103. The discovery that an object, matter, or thing is out of place.
104. An unexpected discovery of an appropriation of money.
105. Paint deliberately or unexpectedly used for concealing something of importance.

A SUSPICIOUS CIRCUMSTANCE
(Continued)

106. A mysterious person has sought transportation facilities.
107. A secreted manuscript comes to light.
108. A person suddenly loses his arrogance.
109. A new atrocity is discovered which has been concealed.
110. Discovery of an unaccountable apology.
111. A person is discovered keeping an appointment after attempting to conceal his plan.
112. The discovery that a person has been blackmailed.
113. The presence of a secret or mysterious cabinet or receptacle is revealed.
114. An effort is made to conceal the use of wine or liquor.
115. A missing bullet, weapon, or other object is discovered.
116. The discovery that a surreptitious assignment has been made.
117. A person attempts to hide himself in an audience.
118. The authenticity of a report or statement or clue is questionable.
119. The investigator hears of a revel which has been kept secret.
120. The disappearance of an important object from the scene of the crime.
121. A delirious person unwittingly makes illuminating statements.
122. An official or other person is demoted or deposed.
123. A person is deserted in trouble.
124. The unexplainable discharge of a person.
125. The discovery that a stage has been set or action staged.
126. An unexpected attack is made.
127. A false report is proved authentic.
128. A person's desire to avenge a wrong is uncovered.
129. The issuance of a strange mandate.
130. In which a person surrounds himself with an unusual defense.
131. A person is fawning or obsequious to another.
132. Report of an unusual noise is revealed.

A SUSPICIOUS CIRCUMSTANCE
(Continued)

133. A person is discovered making an attempt to secrete a weapon or other object.
134. The secret association of a person with the victim or another person.
135. A peculiar assortment of objects has been concealed and is discovered.
136. Discovery of an attachment between some one and the victim or other important character.
137. Disposal of evidence of attack is attempted.
138. An auspicious event is attended by a person under suspicion.
139. The discovery of an autograph or an article which has been secreted.
140. A person who usually retires early is discovered prowling at a late hour.
141. Where a person deliberately misleads or gives misdirecting information.
142. A person supposedly poor is discovered to possess a large amount of money.
143. An attempt on the part of some person to meddle.
144. A person has purposely misinterpreted a message or statement.
145. An attempt to commit murder is discovered.
146. Discovery that a person has lost to the victim in a game.
147. Proof of a person's authority comes to light unexpectedly.
148. A person tries to jump a bail bond.
149. A secret or concealed stairway is discovered.
150. A person is unexpectedly discovered to be a criminal.
151. Discovery that the giving or taking of a bribe has been concealed.
152. An unexplained breach of friendly relations.

A SUSPICIOUS CIRCUMSTANCE
(Continued)

153. A person awakes from a sleep or stupor and speaks what is in his subconscious mind.
154. Audience is given to an unusual person.
155. An attempt has been made to oust or expel a person from a building or a group.
156. It is discovered that persons have strangely decided to remain neutral.
157. The fact that a peculiar offer has been made is uncovered.
158. A person's secret aversion to the victim is revealed.
159. An attempt to conceal a weapon.
160. A comparison of handwriting directs suspicion against a character.
161. A peculiar or marred photograph discovered.
162. Secret return of one or more to scene of crime.
163. A character feigns illness.
164. It is discovered that a suspect is involved in a plot to commit a second crime or murder.
165. A person with certain authority has issued a decree that has aroused antagonism.
166. It is revealed that a character has been ostracised or blackmailed.
167. A person turns panicky at a question or suggestion.
168. The use of a mechanical device has been concealed.
169. Attempt is made to conceal the giving of a narcotic to a person.
170. It is discovered that a picture, motion picture or still, has been taken.
171. Mysterious disappearance of a necessary object in the evidence.
172. A person is discovered to have an obsession about the victim or someone or something of importance.
173. The effort to conceal a bargain is uncovered.

A SUSPICIOUS CIRCUMSTANCE
(Continued)

174. A person thought to have plenty is found to have only the bare necessities.
175. The disappearance of evidence of bargaining.
176. A condition or circumstance forces one to betray himself unawares.
177. Threats of a secret society or sect indicate outside influence.
178. Discovery that a picture has some hidden message.
179. Suspicion is directed to a character by his unexplained outburst of passion.
180. Attempt has been made to prevent the release of an imprisoned person.

OPERATION No. 5

A SUSPICIOUS CIRCUMSTANCE OR BAFFLING SITUATION IS—

LIST C.

1. The discovery of an instrument which indicates evidence to do with the crime.
2. What appears to be a cheap bauble is discovered to be or contain a thing of value.
3. The suspicious imitation of one character of another.
4. Revelation that a man has made love to a woman he hates.
5. A supposedly pious person turns vicious.
6. A person conceals the fact that he is a linguist.
7. Mysterious disappearance of a guard.
8. Insistent declaration of alibi by suspect.
9. An innocent person is strangely decoyed.
10. An attempt to remove bloodstains or other incriminating evidence.
11. The use of an instrument or tool is discovered to have been made.
12. The victim or an important character is discovered to be involved in legal action.
13. An attempt to conceal a person's disgraceful actions.
14. The unexplained disheveled condition of a character arouses suspicion.
15. A distinguished person is found out of usual background.
16. An elopement has been interfered with or prevented.
17. Effort to conceal new type of energy.
18. A doctor proves to be a fake.
19. A barricade which conceals or protects an entrance.
20. Unexpected discovery of the illegitimacy of a child.

A SUSPICIOUS CIRCUMSTANCE
(Continued)

21. A secret attempt to receive a blessing or benediction.
22. Discovery of a password.
23. It is revealed that a guard or patrol has been placed.
24. An attempt to have a person put in a pest-house, sanitarium, or other place of confinement.
25. The misuse of medicine.
26. The discovery of a secret pledge or promise.
27. An illusion or apparition is discovered to have been purposely created.
28. Revelation that a bribe has been offered.
29. It is revealed that immunity has been promised one for a consideration.
30. A strange or unusual weapon is discovered.
31. An attempt to disrupt a meeting.
32. Surprising action of an animal, particularly a dog.
33. An unusual electrical contrivance is discovered.
34. A person is discovered to have a taste for weird or unusual poetry or fiction.
35. Attempted prevention of an endowment.
36. The discovery that one in authority is an imposter.
37. A person is disconcerted when confronted with material evidence.
38. A concealed electric bell, buzzer, or other sound instrument is discovered.
39. A character is discovered to have a questionable reputation.
40. The use of radio, telephone, telegraph, or cable has been concealed and discovered.
41. Attempt to conceal plunder, loot, or property claimed to be one's own.
42. The repeated recurrence of an apparently insignificant action.

A SUSPICIOUS CIRCUMSTANCE
(Continued)

43. It is revealed that a person is secretly financing a person or enterprise.
44. Attempted plagiarism is discovered.
45. A secret rendezvous is discovered.
46. A person conceals evidence of rivalry over a person or issue.
47. A facility is rendered useless.
48. Suspicion is thrown on a member of investigator's family.
49. Mysterious signals appear in various places.
50. Discovery of a peculiar leakage—liquid, liquor, blood, etc.
51. The actions or attitude of a person discovered to be pretense.
52. A striking resemblance of one to another.
53. Unexpected surveillance is discovered.
54. Suspect is only one who had access to premises.
55. A person's prescribed diet has been interfered with.
56. A person is unexpectedly discovered to be an officer or official.
57. An attempt to produce a spirit manifestation.
58. A banished person suddenly—perhaps secretly—appears.
59. A secret visit to bank is discovered.
60. Heart balm is demanded, indicating trouble in love affair.
61. A system of espionage is discovered.
62. A person has falsified a record or other possible evidence.
63. There is a discrepancy in a story told by a character.
64. An object supposedly genuine is discovered to be a fake.
65. An unusual gesture made repeatedly.
66. An effort to belittle another after a show of praising him:
67. The unexpected recipiency of a bequest.
68. A demand for payment of a bill is discovered.
69. Discovery that a character is envious of another.
70. Familiarity with another suddenly ceases.
71. Attempted destruction of a conveyance.

A SUSPICIOUS CIRCUMSTANCE
(Continued)

72. One who hides crooked work behind honorable employment.
73. Attempts to follow another unawares.
74. It is unexpectedly discovered that the victim has blamed a supposedly innocent person for wrongdoing.
75. A suspected person makes a serious blunder.
76. Discovery that there has been a conflict over the awarding of a prize.
77. A person who has bolted is apprehended.
78. The playing of a game repeatedly.
79. Secret opening or compartment discovered in furniture.
80. A person resents an examination.
81. Destruction of an exhibit discovered or prevented.
82. Efforts to start a fire.
83. A hidden brand is unexplainable.
84. The discovery of a concealed or unexplained budget or other financial statement.
85. Discovery of an effort to burn something.
86. An attempt to interfere with an expose.
87. A secret bolt is discovered, with hidden means of being operated—on door, gate, panel, box, etc.
88. Attempt to remove or conceal blood stains is discovered.
89. A person going under a fictitious name.
90. An effort to bully or brow-beat comes to light.
91. The mysterious exchange of presents.
92. The discovery of an essential missing part of an object.
93. Someone has given an overdose of medicine or poisonous drug.
94. Discovery that valuable jewels have been concealed.
95. A mysterious rescue or escape is effected.
96. A message is conveyed in riddle.
97. Suspicion is thrown on investigator himself.

A SUSPICIOUS CIRCUMSTANCE
(Continued)

98. A message written in a strange language is discovered.
99. Mysterious warning received.
100. There is a discrepancy in important dates.
101. Denial of marriage.
102. The giving of a peculiar pledge is discovered.
103. A freak alibi is established.
104. A tool is rendered useless.
105. The unexplained bestowal of a favor.
106. A supposedly conventional person is found to be living a Bohemian life.
107. The disappearance or reappearance of a body guard.
108. Investigator is confronted with living double of murdered victim.
109. A secret room or compartment is discovered.
110. It is discovered that some witness has been influenced to testify falsely.
111. A person fakes blindness and is discovered.
112. A message is found to be a ruse or decoy.
113. Revelation that a woman has accepted the attentions of a man she hates.
114. A person is unexpectdly denounced.
115. An attempt to cause a person to be deported.
116. The discovery that parts of a body have been removed.
117. It is discovered that there has been discord in the family or among the associates of the victim.
118. Discovery that a person has secretly been kept a prisoner.
119. An attempt to bring about a reconciliation.
120. Baggage is discovered to contain mysterious or suspicious object.
121. Deliberate attempt to blame another.

A SUSPICIOUS CIRCUMSTANCE
(Continued)

122. Discovery that favors have been withdrawn.
123. Hiding or destroying food.
124. Discovery of a gift, given or withheld.
125. The destruction of evidence of a party.
126. A person is discovered to be one of a sect or clan.
127. A foreboding is given credence.
128. A person is discovered to have a dual nature.
129. An attempt to take a deposition.
130. The disappearance of a person detailed to seek specific evidence.
131. It is discovered that a person has taken an unnecessary detour.
132. A person is prevented from fulfilling a contract or an agreement, legal or personal.
133. A supposed friend is discovered to be an enemy of the victim or other important person.
134. A hint is contained in a cryptic publication.
135. Unnecessary precaution has been concealed and is discovered.
136. A person is discovered to have been convicted of a crime.
137. It is revealed that there has been a controversy over religious questions.
138. Attempt to conceal the condition of a person's finances.
139. A ballot has been cast, the discovery of which reveals a plot of some sort.
140. Discovery that a person has been banished from a place.
141. Something is discovered that is used as a blind.
142. A person who has been bound or gagged is discovered.
143. The discovery of unexpected bravery or heroism.
144. An object concealed in bread or other food stuff.
145. The similarity of crimes occuring in widely separated places.
146. The mysterious failure of some one to keep a bargain.
147. Body of victim mysteriously disappears.

A SUSPICIOUS CIRCUMSTANCE
(Continued)

148. The discovery that there has been a split in the ranks of the suspects.
149. Important evidence is stolen from investigator.
150. Discovery that a secret code is being used.
151. False signals are used to mislead investigator.
152. A means of communication is mysteriously interrupted.
153. The mysterious failure of some one to keep a tryst.
154. Suspicion is thrown on person known to be dead.
155. The disarming of a person unexpectedly discovered concealing a weapon.
156. A person tries to conceal a fraudulent transaction made with another.
157. A person has asked forgiveness.
158. Discovery that a person has been threatened with prosecution.
159. The concealed kinship of one person with another is discovered.
160. Discovery that a person is bankrupt or attempting to avoid bankruptcy.
161. Second crime of a similar nature occurring in same locality.
162. An attempt is made by a stranger to gain entrance to scene of crime.
163. The presence of a mysterious stranger at or near the scene of the crime.
164. Suspicion is thrown on a person known to be far away.
165. Discovery of a quarrel which participant attempts to conceal.
166. Discovery of suspicious issue of bank drafts or certified checks.
167. A person has concealed the fact that he received a rake-off or bribe, and evidence of same.
168. An attempt to refute a statement.
169. A broken instrument or object is discovered.

A SUSPICIOUS CIRCUMSTANCE
(Continued)

170. A weapon is rendered useless.
171. The use of mysticism either confuses or throws light on a subject.
172. The sudden discovery of drug addiction.
173. An unexplained injury to a person.
174. The sudden breaking down of a person's health.
175. The unexpected recipiency of a bequest.
176. A person turns berserk over question, accusation or incident.
177. Investigator is mystified by weird sounds and appearances in vicinity of scene of crime.
178. An obstacle created by a mechanical device retards operations of investigator.
179. An item in "Personal" column of newspaper conveys veiled information.
180. Investigator is decoyed by woman's cries for help.

OPERATION NO. 6

A THRILLING SITUATION DEVELOPS WHEN

As the story progresses and begins to near the climax, it is always necessary to "speed up" by injecting some thrilling and spectacular action or tense situation which builds up the suspense. The following list provides 180 of such situations. It is suggested that the author use only one of these as to use more would in all probability complicate the plot and perhaps sidetrack the main story thread.

1. There is a murder of a friend of the victim.
2. There is an explosion.
3. The investigator is trapped.
4. There is a plunging into darkness.
5. There is a spectacular rescue.
6. There is a display of primitive passion.
7. There is an outburst of emotion.
8. There is a conflict between sexes.
9. There is a scientific demonstration.
10. There is a spectacular duel.
11. There is a murder of a business associate of the victim.
12. There is a conflagration.
13. There is a storm.
14. There is a spectacular interruption.
15. It is discovered that a supposed corpse is a living person.
16. There is a kidnapping of a friend of the victim.
17. There is a weird or gruesome discovery.
18. There is an embarrassing discovery.
19. There is a threatened murder of a business associate of the victim.
20. There is a spectacular gamble.
21. There is a breakdown.
22. The use of hypnosis is discovered.
23. The discovery that a suspect has a strange mania.
24. A mysterious decoy is located.

A THRILLING SITUATION—
(Continued)

25. Investigator is marooned.
26. There is a murder of a relative of the victim.
27. There is a kidnapping of a relative of the victim.
28. There is a spectacular collapse of a structure.
29. There is a deluge caused.
30. There is a spectacular stunt.
31. There is a fight.
32. There are mysterious and weird sounds.
33. There is a sensational identification.
34. There is a threatened murder of a relative of the victim.
35. There is a carousal.
36. A mystic influence is discovered.
37. A corpse is brought to life.
38. There is a kidnapping of an employee of the victim.
39. A loved one of the investigator is trapped.
40. There is a trail by bloodhounds.
41. There is a murder of an investigator.
42. There is a spectacular collision.
43. There is a riot caused.
44. There is the formation of a mob.
45. There is a sensational or mysterious disguise for some purpose.
46. There is a public denunciation.
47. There is a baffling alibi established.
48. Investigator is drugged or incapacitated.
49. Evidence is destroyed by natural phenomenon.
50. A spectacular event is staged.
51. There is a threatened murder of a servant of the victim.
52. There is an unexpected appearance.
53. There is a mysterious and weird phenomenon.
54. A substitution of persons is effected.

A THRILLING SITUATION—
(Continued)

55. A mysterious place of concealment is discovered.
56. A mysterious suicide is discovered.
57. A suspect commits suicide.
58. A ghastly scene is staged for effect.
59. There is a kidnapping of a servant of the victim.
60. There is a threatened explosion.
61. There is infliction of torture.
62. There is a siege.
63. There is a murder of an employee of the victim.
64. There is an encounter with a maniac.
65. There is a runaway.
66. There is a raid.
67. There is a weird natural phenomenon.
68. There is an unexpected opposition.
69. There is a discovery of an illicit traffic.
70. There is a spiritualistic or psychic manifestation.
71. There is a threatened murder of an employee of the victim.
72. A plot or device to frighten is discovered.
73. The law interferes with the work of the investigator.
74. Reinforcements are delayed.
75. A loved one of the investigator is kidnapped.
76. Evidence of spirit manifestations are encountered.
77. An attempt is made by a mob to rescue a suspect.
78. There is a murder of an investigator.
79. There is a kidnapping of a lover or sweetheart of the victim.
80. There is a threatened infliction of torture.
81. A suspect is trapped.
82. There is an exciting communication or signal.
83. There is a threatened murder of an investigator.
84. There is a seizure.

A THRILLING SITUATION—
(Continued)

85. It becomes necessary to invade a sanctuary.
86. A captive witness is rescued.
87. A fake concession is made.
88. There is a bombardment.
89. There is a spectacular flight.
90. There is a forced entrance.
91. There is a murder of an enemy of the victim.
92. A suspect develops to be another investigator.
93. A thrilling dash is made to prevent destruction of evidence by fire.
94. An attempted lynching is made.
95. There is a threatened murder of an enemy of the victim.
96. There is a panic.
97. There is a spectacular descent or ascent.
98. There is a kidnapping of an investigator.
99. There is an exciting alarm.
100. There is an ambush.
101. There is an accident to a conveyance.
102. A concealed device for murder is discovered.
103. The investigator is captured.
104. There is the appearance of an apparition.
105. There is a murder of a rival of the victim.
106. There is a sensational forgery.
107. There is a spectacular illumination.
108. There is an attempted murder of a decoy.
109. There is a kidnapping of an enemy of the victim.
110. A secret trick entrance or exit is discovered.
111. There is a demonstration.
112. There is a masquerade.
113. There is a weird ceremony.

A THRILLING SITUATION—
(Continued)

114. There is an attack by a vicious animal or reptile.
115. There is a threatened murder of a rival of the victim.
116. A forgery of evidence is discovered.
117. A living person exchanges places with the dead.
118. It is discovered that the victim is other than the one he was supposed to be.
119. The investigator discovers that the suspect is a friend or loved one.
120. There is an inundation.
121. There is a murder of an employer of the victim.
122. There is a kidnapping of a business associate of the victim.
123. There is a sensational jail break.
124. There is a discovery of a strange instrument of wholesale destruction.
125. There is a sensational escape.
126. There is a threatened murder of an employer of the victim.
127. A mysterious method of disposing of the corpse is discovered.
128. A forgery of identification marks is discovered.
129. An innocent suspect is subjected to torture.
130. There is a spectacular voyage.
131. There is an obstruction or blocade.
132. There is a thrilling robbery.
133. There is an exciting or spectacular warning.
134. There is a display of insubordination.
135. There is the discovery of an unknown or mysterious person.
136. There is a kidnapping of a rival of the victim.
137. It is discovered that a supposedly dead person is alive.
138. It is discovered that a supposed investigator is a criminal.
139. It is discovered that a woman has been employed to trap suspect.

A THRILLING SITUATION—
(Continued)

140. A barricade is erected by a suspect.
141. The disastrous use of chemicals is prevented.
142. There is a murder of a lover or sweetheart of the victim.
143. There is a kidnapping of an employer of the victim.
144. A suspect suddenly becomes mentally deranged.
145. Witness about to disclose information is killed by accident.
146. Evidence is discovered that an organized criminal gang is involved.
147. An attack is made by a ferocious trained animal.
148. There is a threatened murder of a lover or sweetheart of the victim.
149. A heathen ceremony takes place.
150. The use of electricity is brought into play.
151. There is a threatened murder of a friend of the victim.
152. There is a spectacular pursuit.
153. There is a sensational forgery.
154. There is a wholesale slaughter.
155. There is an attempted murder.
156. A witness is subjected to torture.
157. There is a murder of an important witness.
158. It has been discovered that a mock ceremony has been performed.
159. A disassociated mystery or crime is solved accidentally.
160. Investigator's operations are handicapped by a rival.
161. A blackmailer threatens to handicap investigation.
162. It is discovered that a huge hoax has been perpetrated.
163. The wrath of a cult is aroused.
164. There is the murder of a stool pigeon.
165. There is a sensational attempt made to discredit the investigator.

A THRILLING SITUATION—
(Continued)

166. A spectacular attempt is made to gain possession of a body.
167. There is an abduction of an important witness.
168. It is discovered that a mechanical method has been employed to simulate the presence of a person.
169. It becomes necessary to encounter great danger in the pursuit of a suspect.
170. A spectacular attempt is made to murder a man who has already been killed.
171. It is discovered that a child has been employed to trap a suspect.
172. It is threatened to involve investigator with suspicion.
173. The presence of some virulent disease or germ is discovered.
174. An attempt is made to precipitate a catastrophe.
175. A new and terrible scientific weapon is used.
176. A pursuit for an old crime or offense interferes.
177. There is a spectacular pursuit to silence a witness.
178. It is discovered that a suspect is an escaped convict.
179. The investigator's disguise is penetrated.
180. There is the discovery that a picture conceals a secret hiding place for valuables.

OPERATION NO. 7

THE SOLUTION IS PRECIPITATED WHEN

We now reach the climax in the story although not the last operation in this Formula. The following list provides the author with 180 solutions to the crime or mystery and of course only one should be used.

1. There is a thrilling pursuit and capture.
2. Criminal is led into a trap.
3. The presence of twins or triplets occasions confusion.
4. There is a forced confession.
5. Criminal is led to believe that accomplices have betrayed him.
6. Vengeance is wrought against criminal by an old enemy.
7. Criminal is permitted to escape when it develops that he or she is a loved one.
8. The guilty party makes a sacrifice for an ideal and confesses.
9. Startling revelations show the criminal to have been a victim of circumstances.
10. It develops that the guilty party is a kinsman and is sacrificed.
11. The guilty party confesses to have murdered or wronged a person by mistake.
12. A confession is forced by the remorse of the guilty party.
13. The guilty party is identified because of an indiscretion.
14. An innocent person confesses a crime to protect another.
15. The guilty person is identified when discovered to be the leader in a revolt.
16. It develops that the crime was either one of self-defense or justifiable.
17. A criminal pursued and slain is discovered to be a kinsman.
18. The guilty party surrenders in obedience to a religious belief.
19. A dog or other animal leads the way to the guilty person.
20. The criminal is apprehended through the efforts of a loved one to protect him.

THE SOLUTION
(Continued)

21. A person believed to be absent is found to be present.
22. An unrecognized person who has been befriended by the suspect in the past comes to his rescue and identifies the guilty person.
23. A vital object which plays an important part in the story develops to be other than it was thought to be.
24. The guilty person is frightened into surrender by what appears to be an occult or spiritual manifestation.
25. It develops that a young child proves an important witness.
26. A supposedly insane or imbecile person proves to be normal and supplies the solution.
27. Police surround hiding place of suspect and effect his capture.
28. The discovery is made that there has been a mistake in the identity of a character.
29. A horrible revenge planned by the guilty person recoils on him and enmeshes him.
30. The criminal in disguise is brought face to face with the person whom he is impersonating.
31. The guilty person is betrayed by one of the opposite sex whose love has been scorned.
32. Rivals come face to face and each accuses the other of the crime.
33. Criminal falls into trap which he has himself set.
34. The positions of an innocent suspect and the guilty person are unexpectedly reversed.
35. The criminal is identified by a brand of tobacco or liquor.
36. The criminal is identified because of having practiced a deception.
37. There has been a supreme match of endurance between investigator and the guilty person.

THE SOLUTION
(Continued)

38. The guilty person is discovered and captured by the occurrence of an unexpected accident.
39. A trivial or unnoticed thing discloses evidence that solves the problem.
40. Evidence is found on the person of an escaping suspect which proves his guilt.
41. A new and powerful weapon is brought into play against the guilty person.
42. A novel methed is used to signal for help.
43. A cripple unexpectedly comes to the aid of the investigator.
44. The criminal is suddenly stricken with a fatal illness and a confession is made.
45. The guilty person is brought down by an attack from a venomous insect or reptile.
46. The criminal is identified by a certain habit.
47. It is discovered that a person believed dead is really alive.
48. Officers intercept escape of criminals.
49. The criminal is identified by tracks.
50. A friend in disguise saves the day for the innocent suspect and identifies the criminal.
51. It is discovered that a character in the story has a dual personality.
52. Officer turns tables on criminal, traps him and forces a confession.
53. An important discovery in connection with the time element is made which aids materially in the capture of the criminal.
54. The fourth degree is used. (Mental anxiety.)
55. A secret mechanical or automatic apparatus is discovered.
56. It is discovered that the stage has been cleverly set.

THE SOLUTION
(Continued)

57. It is discovered that the guilty person was employed by the victim himself to commit the crime.

58. It is discovered that the supposed victim is in reality the criminal.

59. An innocent suspect is saved and the criminal apprehended by the timely arrival of reinforcements.

60. The criminal is exposed by last minute testimony introduced in Court.

61. Hypnotism is used to disclose important evidence or bring about a confession.

62. A person under the influence of liquor discloses himself to be the criminal.

63. The criminal is identified as a result of a hunch on the part of the investigator.

64. It is discovered that a suspect is a somnambulist.

65. The guilty party makes a sacrifice for a loved one and surrenders.

66. The criminal is identified as a mad man.

67. Use is made of a new invention or scientific discovery.

68. It is discovered that the chief witness against an innocent suspect is mentally deranged.

69. A character in dire need of a drug is brought to confess himself as the criminal.

70. The criminal, who has been believed to be a loved one, proves to be an enemy in disguise.

71. A chain of mysterious or tragic events is staged by a clever detective or investigator, in order to discover a solution to a crime or problem.

72. There is an attempt made by the suspect to decoy the investigator away.

THE SOLUTION
(Continued)

73. The criminal is besieged until he surrenders.
74. Torture is used to force a confession from a guilty person.
75. The presence of a cleverly arranged secret hiding place is discovered to have been provided by the suspect.
76. The third degree is used.
77. An apparently impregnable alibi is destroyed.
78. The investigator tricks the criminal into pursuing him.
79. A confession is made by an accomplice of the criminal.
80. Bloodhounds are used in trailing the criminal, leading to his capture.
81. A guilty suspect subconsciously reacts the crime.
82. A mysterious apparatus is discovered in the possession of a suspect.
83. A guilty person is tricked into making an admission which reveals him as the perpetrator of the crime.
84. A suspect in endeavoring to clear himself of suspicion in one crime unknowingly confesses to another.
85. Poison or gas is used to dislodge a guilty suspect and bring about his capture and confession.
86. A too-talkative or boastful person brings about his own apprehension for commission of the crime.
87. Mental telepathy is used in the solution of the crime.
88. A person under great mental stress reveals himself to be the criminal.
89. It is discovered that the chief witness against an innocent suspect has a personal grudge and is protecting the guilty party who may be himself or another.
90. The criminal is exposed by his participation in an orgy.
91. The criminal, cornered, commits suicide.
92. In an attempt to escape, the criminal is killed by accident.

THE SOLUTION
(Continued)

93. A suspect is discovered prowling at night.
94. The criminal is revealed by a peculiarity in his voice or laugh.
95. A suspect, confronted with indisputable evidence of his crime, or by the dead body of his victim, becomes wild and loses control of himself, thereby exposing his guilt.
96. The criminal is apprehended when he is deserted by his friends.
97. The criminal is identified and captured on account of his efforts to remove a cache.
98. The criminal is identified when articles of disguise are discovered in his possession.
99. The criminal is identified when a note written by the victim comes to light.
100. The identity of the criminal is identified and located by trailing a sweetheart or lover.
101. The identity of the criminal is established by a dictaphone record.
102. It is discovered that a door, gate, lid, or other protection has been forced.
103. The criminal is led to believe that an accomplice or loved one has been captured.
104. A guilty suspect returns to the scene of the crime.
105. A criminal is identified and captured through his efforts to remove incriminating evidence or an eye witness.
106. It develops that a suspect has been guilty of producing weird effects to frighten others.
107. A criminal in his efforts to plant suspicion on an innocent one unconsciously incriminates himself.
108. Bound witness left to burn is rescued by officers and identifies criminal.

THE SOLUTION
(Continued)

109. Superstitious fear causes a person to reveal himself as the criminal.
110. The identity of the criminal is disclosed by the tracing of mysterious threats that are received by the investigator.
111. The criminal, believing everything to be lost, makes a voluntary confession.
112. Unusual activity on the part of the suspect discloses him as the criminal.
113. Fear of the elements or destruction by a catastrophe causes a criminal to disclose his identity.
114. The very novelty of the concealment of the evidence of the crime arouses suspicion and leads to the apprehension and identification of the criminal.
115. The nervous actions of a character lead to the discovery of the criminal.
116. The identity of the criminal is revealed through someone talking in his sleep.
117. The discovery is made of a strange alliance or relationship between persons.
118. The criminal is identified by his efforts to change his appearance by plastic surgery, mutilation, or otherwise.
119. It is discovered that a suspect has made plans for a quick getaway.
120. An apparently respectable and honored person is discovered in a questionable place.
121. In an attempt to escape the criminal is killed by the investigator.
122. A peculiar speech formula or stereotyped word signal is overheard between suspects.

THE SOLUTION
(Continued)

123. The identity of the criminal is established by a dictograph record.
124. A witness is tortured to force him to disclose the identity of the criminal.
125. A criminal is identified and captured in his efforts to produce evidence favorable to himself.
126. The discovery of a bound and gagged missing witness in a secret room leads to the disclosure and capture of the criminal.
127. The discovery of secret panels, concealed places of entrance and exit, underground tunnels, etc., leads to the capture of the criminals.
128. Weapons, drugs, or other paraphernalia are discovered in the possession of the suspect.
129. There is an attempt on the part of the suspect to commit another crime.
130. The investigator overhears the babblings of a weak-minded person.
131. An award is given to another criminal to induce him to disclose the identity or location of the guilty person.
132. Part of a body or a portion of the spoils is found in the possession of the suspect.
133. Investigation into the activities of one higher up in the criminal world leads to the identity and disclosure of the criminal.
134. The mysterious illness of a person is investigated.
135. A suspect is suddenly confronted by a person whom he believes to be absent or dead.
136. The identity of the criminal is revealed by his effort to commit suicide.
137. It is discovered that a suspect is allied with or under obligation to a secret order or cult.

THE SOLUTION
(Continued)

138. The discovery is made of the unexplained injury to a person.
139. The discovery is made of an attempt to conceal acquaintance-ship or friendship between persons.
140. It is discovered that a suspect has taken unusual precautions to protect himself.
141. The discovery is made of a strange or novel weapon in the possession of a person.
142. The criminal is revealed by the use of peculiar methods which are known to be exclusively his own.
143. There is an attempt of a person to create the impression that he has been killed or done away with.
144. It develops that a suspect has been connected with some previous crime.
145. A suspect is caught attempting to dispose of evidence.
146. A suspect is discovered to have purposely injured himself.
147. It is discovered that some character has been making wanton expenditures of money.
148. It is discovered that the victim has been the object of vengeance on the part of barbarians or savages.
149. It is learned that a suspect is a devotee of voodooism, black magic, or other weird beliefs.
150. A suspect suddenly turns berserk over a question, accusation, or incident.
151. The discovery is made that the suspect has been faking blindness.
152. The criminal is discovered and apprehended through the use of modern scientific methods.
153. The discovery is made that a supposedly helpless person has some strange means of locomotion.
154. The discovery is made that some character, who knows that his

THE SOLUTION
(Continued)

days are numbered, has a strange grudge.

155. The apprehension of the criminal is secured through the lure of a beautiful woman.

156. It is revealed that a suspect has made a previous attempt on the life of the victim.

157. The identity of the criminal is revealed through evidence discovered when there is renovation, cleaning out, clearing up, draining, or rearrangment of a room, vault, container, or other place.

158. The identity of the criminal is revealed by the discovery of a symbol which he has left.

159. It is discovered that a suspect has been masquerading as one of the opposite sex.

160. The criminal is identified through a peculiar eccentricity which he has.

161. It is discovered that a suspect has destroyed a means of defense or protection.

162. The capture of the guilty person is facilitated by the forces of Nature, such as an earthquake, tornado, flood, or other natural phenomenon.

163. Aid is obtained through the efforts of an old woman.

164. The intended murder of investigator is frustrated by interference of one who has been suspected.

165. It is discovered that a suspect has the characteristics of a sadist.

166. It is discovered that a character is concealing a scar or other physical deformity which provides a mark of identification.

167. It is learned that a suspect is a hypnotic subject.

168. A slight mistake in the plans of the criminal reveals the truth and results in his capture or death.

169. There is an attempt made by the suspect to kill the investigator.

THE SOLUTION
(Continued)

170. The fortified hiding place of the criminal is attacked and destroyed.
171. The discovery is made that the suspect, who is supposed to be a cripple, has been faking.
172. The discovery is made that a character has decided to end his days at some time in the near future.
173. It is discovered that a suspect has been lying as to his actions or whereabouts.
174. The identity of the criminal is revealed by a threat which he has made.
175. The criminal is identified by a peculiar walk, or other revealing characteristic.
176. It is discovered that a suspect has attempted to cause a serious accident.
177. Investigator exposes himself and suspect to what looks like imminent death, in order to secure confession.
178. It develops that a high official connected with the prosecution of the case is the criminal.
179. Captured suspect voluntarily confesses because of erroneous belief that investigator held conclusive evidence of his guilt.
180. It is discovered that the victim brought about his own death for the purpose of being revenged on the suspect who is believed guilty.

OPERATION 8.

THE GUILTY ONE IS

This list provides the author with a description of the guilty party. It will be observed that there are a number of repetitions and these have been made purposely. One of the rules in writing the modern scientific detective-mystery story is that not only the victim but the guilty person also must be some colorful character and not just an ordinary person or criminal. Particularly should the guilty person be one who would not be ordinarily suspected.

Inasmuch as there are 180 numbers on the Robot disc it was necessary to make repetitions on this list in order to confine it to colorful characters. It should be borne in mind that the guilty person, whoever he or she develops to be, must have been on the scene from the beginning of the story and possibly has been considered as a suspect. This is one of the cardinal principles which must be observed as it is not permissible to introduce such a character at or near the end of the story.

1. A dramatic critic.
2. A kinswoman.
3. A reformer.
4. A consul.
5. An underworld queen.
6. A public official.
7. A female mystic.
8. A capitalist.
9. An executive.
10. A plastic surgeon.
11. A dancer.
12. A courier.
13. A manikin.
14. A playwright.
15. A showman.
16. An exporter.
17. An architect.
18. A trusted employee.
19. A ringmaster.
20. A philanthropist.
21. A ship owner.
22. A banker.
23. A female sports star.
24. A radical.
25. An engineer.
26. A woman editor.
27. A spy.
28. A beauty specialist.
29. A hypnotist.
30. An Oriental.
31. A scholar.
32. A society belle.
33. An explorer.
34. A jealous lover or sweetheart.
35 A professor,
36. A bondsman.
37. A chorus girl.
38. An interpreter.
39. A bon vivant.
40. A woman librarian.
41. An apostle of a new sect.
42. A gambler.
43. An artist.
44. A sportsman.

THE GUILTY ONE
(Continued)

45. An author.
46. A candidate.
47. An old servant.
48. A clerk.
49. A psychologist.
50. A woman attorney.
51. A probation officer.
52. A dictator.
53. A pseudo-noblewoman.
54. A motion picture director.
55. A clown.
56. A doctor,
57. A model.
58. A spiritualist.
59. An impresario.
60. A curio collector.
61. A captain.
62. A scientist.
63. An editor.
64. A hermit.
65. A caretaker.
66. A florist.
67. A promotor.
68. A woman philanthropist.
69. A former friend.
70. A government official.
71. A bacteriologist.
72. A pawnbroker.
73. A woman judge.
74. A gigolo.
75. A manufacturer.
76. A reformer.
77. A modiste.
78. A woman artist.
79. A paramour.
80. A broker.
81. An artist.
82. A banker.
83. A sculptor.
84. A woman school teacher.
85. A prosecutor.
86. A contractor.
87. A housekeeper.
88. A publisher.
89. A financier.
90. An aviation executive.
91. A trader.
92. A woman sculptor.
93. A politician.
94. A hotel keeper.
95. A radio announcer.
96. A merchant.
97. A kinsman.
98. A judge.
99. An administrator.
100. A racketeer.
101. An inventor.
102. A chorus girl.
103. An autocrat.
104. A bigot.

THE GUILTY ONE
(Continued)

105. A gambler.
106. A private secretary.
107. A bon vivant.
108. A chemist.
109. A model.
110. A family lawyer.
111. An attorney.
112. A professor.
113. A gambler.
114. An Egyptologist.
115. A manikin.
116. A trophy hunter.
117. A captain.
118. A countess.
119. An auctioneer.
120. An animal fancier.
121. A scientist.
122. A clown.
123. A doctor.
124. A curio collector.
125. A photographer.
126. An architect.
127. A woman artist.
128. A motion picture director.
129. A dramatic critic.
130. A female settlement worker.
131. A bootlegger.
132. A politician.
133. A junk dealer.
134. A translator.
135. A society belle.
136. A foreign doctor.
137. A governess.
138. An engineer.
139. A dictator.
140. A merchant.
141. An actress.
142. A neighbor.
143. A rancher.
144. An archæologist.
145. A broker.
146. A statesman.
147. A publisher.
148. An accountant.
149. A manufacturer.
150. A woman librarian.
151. A capitalist.
152. A dancer.
153. A juror.
154. A motion picture actor.
155. A paramour.
156. A radio artist.
157. A pseudo-nobleman.
158. A woman nurse.
159. A palmist.
160. A hypnotist.
161. A student.
162. An antiques collector.
163. A rival.
164. A mystic.

THE GUILTY ONE
(Continued)

165. An actor.
166. A female spy.
167. A caretaker.
168. A woman probation officer.
169. A sportsman.
170. A chorus girl.
171. A woman spiritualist.
172. A motion picture producer.
173. A musician.
174. A female entertainer.
175. A psychologist.
176. An inventor.
177. A rejected lover or discarded sweetheart.
178. A botanist.
179. A lobbyist.
180. An auctioneer.

OPERATION 9

THE MOTIVE IS

A part of the climax in the modern detective-mystery story is the discovery of the motive for the commission of the crime simultaneously with the apprehension of the criminal. Therefore as a matter of fact, the climax in this formula embraces all three of these last operations—the solution, the guilty person, and the motive.

There are three lists of motives but the author should use only one, unless he is able to dial or select another which fits in properly with it. The method of determining which of these lists to use is described in the General Directions in the front of the book.

LIST A

1. The enforcement of the abandonment of a project.
2. To escape from abdication or banishment.
3. Because of unrequited love.
4. Vengeance against a deserter.
5. The discovery of the whereabouts of a den.
6. To silence an accuser.
7. To gain possession of arms.
8. Vengeance against one who has debased one.
9. The desire to produce a phenomenon.
10. To escape the payment of a lost wager.
11. To secure life insurance.
12. To escape from an repression.
13. To destroy an infatuation.
14. The disrupting of an organization.
15. Vengeance against a deceiver.
16. To be rid of hypnotic influence.
17. To avoid jurisdiction.
18. To facilitate an escape.
19. The prevention of an imitation.
20. To satisfy a horoscope.
21. Vengeance against one who has humbled one's pride.
22. The avoidance of an accusation.

THE MOTIVE IS
(Continued)

23. To settle a dispute.
24. To possess an abode.
25. To escape from a master.
26. To prevent adultery.
27. Vengeance against a representative of the law.
28. To avoid shame.
29. To get relief from a monstrosity or abomination.
30. The facilitating of a financial transaction.
31. The prevention of a conspiracy.
32. To withdraw from a bargain.
33. Vengeance against one who is guilty of hounding.
34. To prevent an expose.
35. To prevent the granting of a concession.
36. To prevent an enemy's obtaining aid.
37. Vengeance against one who has brought injustice.
38. Escaping from bondage.
39. The prevention of an injustice.
40. Fear of a previous crime's being discovered.
41. The satisfaction of an impulse.
42. Vengeance against one who has aroused hatred against a friend or loved one.
43. To prevent sabotage.
44. The escape from a vicious motive.
45. The enforcement of allegiance.
46. The penetration of a camouflage or disguise.
47. The punishment of a bigamist.
48. To escape expatriation or exile.
49. To protect one's family.
50. The desire to obtain pay for services or possessions.

THE MOTIVE IS
(Continued)

51. To escape a carousal.
52. Vengeance against one who has given insult to a clan.
53. The prevention of bribery.
54. Escaping from repudiation or dishonor.
55. The seeking to obtain the solution to a scientific experiment.
56. To predetermine destiny.
57. Vengeance against one who has brought dishonor.
58. The satisfaction of anger.
59. To prevent the destruction of one's property or fortune.
60. Because of excessive grief.
61. To obtain an exoneration.
62. The prevention of a "frameup".
63. To escape intimidation.
64. Vengeance against one who is guilty of abuse to a loved one.
65. To avoid a confession.
66. The enforcement of authority.
67. The ambition to obtain gold.
68. To be removed from degradation.
69. To serve as a rebuke or an intimidation.
70. To escape infection.
71. The punishment of one who is guilty of arrogance or tyranny.
72. Prevention of bigamy.
73. Anxiety to obtain immunity.
74. To secure a legacy or inheritance.
75. The enforcement of an adjustment or reimbursement.
76. Jealous revenge.
77. To be relieved from an annoyance.
78. To escape from the results of an accident.
79. To avenge a wrong or insult, either real or fancied.
80. The avoiding of discovery.

THE MOTIVE IS
(Continued)

81. Vengeance against one who has caused mental agony to a loved one.
82. To justify a fatalism.
83. The avoidance of a conflict.
84. Because one is refused forgiveness.
85. The prevention of a revolt.
86. Vengeance against one who has threatened an expose.
87. To avoid paying a penalty.
88. To avenge a suicide.
89. To establish a precedent as a hero.
90. The prevention of an alienation.
91. To satisfy an abnormal appetite.
92. To possess affection.
93. Vengeance against an insulter.
94. The satisfaction of an antipathy.
95. To escape a death warrant.
96. The ambition to obtain possession of an inheritance.
97. To prevent the sacrifice of a good name.
98. To avoid the fate of an outcast.
99. Vengeance against one who has brought calamity to a loved one or friend.
100. To escape a commission.
101. To prevent contagion.
102. The necessity to defend one's honor or the honor of one's family.
103. To remove an ill-omen.
104. The effort to obtain a drug or a restorative.
105. To rescue a loved one.
106. The undermining of a system.
107. Vengeance against one who has caused physical agony.
108. To escape an abhorrent situation.

THE MOTIVE IS
(Continued)

109. The prevention of an alarm.
110. To emphasize a protest or serve as an example.
111. To avoid physical injury.
112. To bring about an arbitration.
113. To yield to an hereditary influence.
114. The desire to bring about a miracle.
115. Vengeance against the robber of a friend.
116. To remove a tabu.
117. The prevention of a disaster.
118. The punishment of perjury.
119. The hope of winning love.
120. To settle a quarrel.
121. The prevention of a murder.
122. Vengeance against a scandal-monger.
123. The prevention of mobilization.
124. To escape the results of folly.
125. Hatred for superiority of other.
126. To escape from an entanglement.
127. To avoid disfiguration.
128. Fear of the discovery of the rifling of an estate.
129. Vengeance against a seditionist.
130. The defeating of a plot.
131. To escape financial obligation.
132. The promotion of the interests of a caste.
133. To prevent a waste of one's fortune.
134. The punishment of a fiend.
135. To remove obstacle to happiness.
136. To be a victim of an obsession.
137. To yield to an inferiority complex.
138. The obtaining of the custody of another person.

THE MOTIVE IS
(Continued)

139. Vengeance against an absconder.
140. The achievement of a place of command.
141. To avoid an enforced association.
142. To prevent the sacrifice of a loved one.
143. To discover a cache or treasure.
144. To avoid disgrace or humiliation.
145. The punishment of one who is avaricious.
146. To bring about a betrothal.
147. The punishment of deception.
148. Activity in behalf of a brotherhood.
149. To serve as an obstacle against an encroachment.
150. The punishment of one who is guilty of brutality.
151. The unwritten law.
152. To obtain a valuable concession.
153. To avoid disqualification.
154. To prevent a favor's being granted.
155. The desire to intercept a message.
156. The enforcing of a confession.
157. To substitute oneself for rightful heir to estate.
158. Vengeance against a seducer.
159. To secure a reprieve.
160. The upholding of a tradition.
161. Because one is refused promotion.
162. To prevent a nomination or an election.
163. To escape a moral obligation.
164. The desire to obtain possession of a key.
165. To avoid boycott.
166. Vengeance against one who threatens to disclose an identity.
167. To prevent the progress of a project.
168. To gain possession of a map.

THE MOTIVE IS
(Continued)

169. Vengeance against one who has brought disfiguration to a loved one.
170. To escape an evil influence.
171. The desire to win notoriety.
172. The aspiration to possess an emblem.
173. To escape a monster.
174. The anxiety to secure necessary evidence.
175. Vengeance against one who has threatened a loved one.
176. To escape servitude.
177. To obtain an acquital.
178. To prevent an answer's being given.
179. Long standing jealousy and envy.
180. The obtaining of money.

OPERATION 9

THE MOTIVE IS—

LIST B.

1. To bring about an adjustment of money matters, or an estate.
2. To get rid of an accomplice.
3. To prevent a rescue.
4. The possession of alcohol.
5. Vengeance against one who has caused mental agony.
6. To eliminate a rival in love.
7. The prevention of a revolution.
8. To protect the good name of a loved one.
9. To escape reproach or revilement.
10. The desire to possess arms.
11. Because one has refused an allowance.
12. The possession of an apparatus.
13. Vengeance against one who has brought dishonor to a loved one.
14. To prevent an abduction.
15. To escape responsibility.
16. To prevent an affiliation.
17. The prevention of a sacrifice of material wealth.
18. To obtain an antidote.
19. Vengeance against one who has brought disgrace and ruin.
20. To escape ostracism.
21. To provide or obtain bail.
22. To remedy a mal-administration.
23. To stop an adventurer.
24. To avoid destruction.
25. To prove strength or power.
26. Vengeance against the abductor of a loved one.
27. To identify an unknown.
28. The prevention of perjury.

THE MOTIVE IS
(Continued)

29. Because of infatuation.
30. The removal of a scourge.
31. To obey a pagan rite.
32. The enforcement of a resignation.
33. Because of temporary insanity.
34. Vengeance against one who has brought death to a loved one.
35. To satisfy radicalism.
36. To divert investigation.
37. To escape a vicious influence.
38. The desire to possess a castle.
39. The satisfaction of pride.
40. The avoidance of physical pain.
41. To establish legitimacy.
42. The punishment of one who is guilty of brutality.
43. Envy of another's good fortune and happiness.
44. The prevention of a hoax.
45. The desire to conceal one's identity.
46. The pursuit of one by an apparition.
47. To prevent a broken heart.
48. The ambition to obtain a formula.
49. To avoid a disorganization.
50. Vengeance against a tyrant.
51. To get relief from an abuse.
52. To escape indictment.
53. The desire to satisfy a habit.
54. The prevention of burglary.
55. To be relieved from danger.
56. To obtain a password.
57. The satisfaction of a desire.
58. To prevent giving away a secret.
59. To escape from criticism.

THE MOTIVE IS
(Continued)

60. Because foul play is suspected.
61. To guarantee a privilege.
62. To satisfy a fascination.
63. An insatiable desire to gain fame.
64. To escape annihilation.
65. The punishment of one who has caused heartbreak to a friend.
66. To be rid of contraband.
67. The prevention of an assembly.
68. To avoid delay.
69. The enforcement of a division of spoils.
70. To win fame.
71. To escape trial.
72. Vengeance against one who has given insult to a loved one.
73. To escape abandonment.
74. To avoid disgrace.
75. The satisfaction of free love.
76. To prevent the sacrifice of a position.
77. To be rid of or obtain revenge against an accuser.
78. To avoid capitulation.
79. Vengeance against one who has brought injustice to a loved one.
80. To conceal or protect an idolatry.
81. The satisfaction of jealousy.
82. The ambition to possess precious metals.
83. To avoid hostility.
84. The desire to obtain a prize.
85. Vengeance against a mental monster.
86. To escape enticement.
87. To satisfy a foreboding.
88. The obtaining of one's liberty.
89. To avoid a confession.

THE MOTIVE IS
(Continued)

90. Vengeance against the murderer of a loved one.
91. To avoid disfiguration.
92. To remove an aggravation or persecution.
93. The enforcing of obedience.
94. The prevention of an unhappy marriage.
95. To satisfy a medium.
96. A reprisal for a vicious act committed by another.
97. To escape from or avenge a memory.
98. To escape being abandoned.
99. To prevent a celebration.
100. The enforcement of an allotment.
101. To escape a family obligation.
102. The demand to enforce a prohibition.
103. To escape insanity.
104. Vengeance against the winner of a wager.
105. The satisfaction of a superstition.
106. The avoidance of trickery.
107. The desire to obtain costly raiment.
108. The prevention of a holdup.
109. To obtain or carry out a strange ritual.
110. Vengeance against one who has demanded suicide of him.
111. To escape being a pawn.
112. To get rid of an aggressor.
113. The hope of obtaining proof of one's statement or decision.
114. To cause apprehension.
115. The attainment of luxury.
116. To avoid a sure defeat.
117. The punishment of a carnalist.
118. To avoid bankruptcy.
119. The prevention of an infringement.
120. To obtain probation.

THE MOTIVE IS
(Continued)

121. To divert a bequest.
122. To gain refuge.
123. Vengeance against the deserter of a loved one.
124. Desire to throw suspicion on enemy or rival.
125. The shielding of another.
126. To escape birthright.
127. The acquisition of a large following.
128. To avoid or prevent a betrayal.
129. Vengeance against one who threatens to expose the weakness of a loved one or friend.
130. To escape discipline.
131. To avoid a deadlock.
132. The enforcement of a decision to one's advantage.
133. The desire to provide incentive for accomplishment.
134. To prevent a desertion.
135. The ambition to gain wealth or fame.
136. Vengeance against one who has given insult to a religion.
137. The prevention of graft.
138. To satisfy the unwritten law.
139. To obtain possession of a domain.
140. To be rid of a hateful person.
141. To obtain a strange weapon.
142. Because one has been set upon by a vicious animal.
143. Vengeance against one who is guilty of abuse.
144. To avoid condemnation.
145. To escape ejection.
146. To satisfy æstheticism.
147. To avoid dispossession.
148. The desire to obtain possession of a valuable gem.
149. Vengeance against a destroyer.
150. Because one has brought anxiety.

THE MOTIVE IS
(Continued)

151. Gaining possession of a business.
152. The enforcement of discipline.
153. To avoid an examination.
154. The accomplishment of a disguise.
155. Vengeance against a betrayer of one's confidence.
156. To obtain immunity.
157. The necessity to make a test.
158. To avoid dishonor.
159. Vengeance against one who has brought banishment to a loved one or friend.
160. The settling of a feud.
161. To escape guilt.
162. The necessity to protect one's home.
163. The prevention of immorality.
164. To bring about an intercession.
165. The solving of a mystery.
166. To cover up illegal or criminal transactions.
167. To avoid humiliation.
168. To satisfy fanaticism.
169. The prevention of an agitation.
170. The enforcement of justice.
171. Vengeance against one who has caused hunger.
172. To prove one's devotion.
173. The need to obtain judgement.
174. To punish an infidel or a defiler.
175. Vengeance against one who has brought disfiguration.
176. To remove subterfuge.
177. Freedom from coercion.
178. Vengeance against one who has deprived one of luxury.
179. To escape acquiescence.
180. To escape asphyxiation.

OPERATION 9

THE MOTIVE IS—

LIST C.

1. The protection of one's good name.
2. To possess an antique.
3. To avoid being a victim of rule, decree, or custom.
4. The securing of approval.
5. Vengeance against one who has debased a loved one.
6. To imitate another.
7. Because one has brought ill health.
8. To force the abandonment of a campaign.
9. The aim to possess certain equipment.
10. The will to remove what seems invincible.
11. Vengeance against one who has attempted to bring death to a loved one.
12. The ambition to swing an election.
13. To obtain advancement.
14. The punishment of a stool-pigeon.
15. The enforcement of a marriage.
16. The possession of an animal.
17. Vengeance against one who has brought calamity.
18. To facilitate bribery.
19. The desire to prove one's courage.
20. To satisfy a bestial instinct.
21. To avenge the death of a comrade.
22. To escape from a demon.
23. Vengeance against one who threatens to perform a miracle or phenomenon.
24. The inauguration of a probe into a serious complication.
25. To provide or motivate a romance.

THE MOTIVE IS
(Continued)

26. To escape disability.
27. To obtain possession of a chemical or a chemical formula.
28. To avoid dishonor.
29. Vengeance against one who has caused physical agony to a loved one.
30. The possession of a rare and valuable thing.
31. To make an example.
32. To head off an expedition.
33. To obtain a license.
34. The prevention of an injury.
35. The punishment of one who has caused heartbreak.
36. To rescue a loved one from vicious attentions.
37. To stop an adventuress.
38. To be rid of an imposition.
39. To prove one's birthright.
40. Being a victim of insanity.
41. Vengeance against one who has aroused hatred.
42. To indulge a criminal impulse.
43. To escape from black magic.
44. To obtain a reconciliation.
45. To avoid corruption.
46. The prevention of homicide.
47. Vengeance against one who threatens to expose his weakness.
48. To be relieved from an encumbrance.
49. To avoid a dangerous experiment.
50. To unearth a secret.
51. To escape espionage.
52. To relieve fear.
53. Vengeance against one who has brought terror.
54. Because of professional jealousy.

THE MOTIVE IS
(Continued)

55. To avoid an assessment.
56. To be rid of a fortune-hunter.
57. Because one has made a farce of what is a tragedy to another.
58. Because an apology has been refused.
59. Vengeance against one who has given insult to a country.
60. The settlement of a dispute.
61. The aiding of a fugitive.
62. To achieve the accomplishment of a purpose.
63. To escape from an abnormality.
64. To escape a barbarian.
65. To effect or produce an alibi.
66. To escape the toils of capitalism.
67. Vengeance against an adulterer.
68. To escape mental agony.
69. The prevention of an affiliation.
70. The craving to obtain possession of a fortune.
71. The attempt to be rid of a pernicious habit.
72. To escape association with a brute.
73. Vengeance against an abductor.
74. The avoidance of an agitation.
75. To escape from a physical malady.
76. The determination to decipher a code.
77. To prevent the arousing of animosity.
78. To satisfy curiosity.
79. To prevent the indulgence of a passion.
80. To escape the necessity of giving an answer.
81. The humiliation of the aristocracy.
82. To settle an argument.
83. The prevention of a calamity.
84. To investigate supernaturalism.

THE MOTIVE IS
(Continued)

85. Vengeance against one who has brought disgrace to a loved one.
86. To escape brutality.
87. To possess accoutrements.
88. To avoid an attachment.
89. To get relief from boredom.
90. To possess beauty.
91. Vengeance against one who has caused banishment.
92. Because of mistaken identity.
93. To escape the surveillance of another.
94. To obtain possession of a talisman.
95. To escape a command.
96. To avoid capture.
97. While a victim of somnambulism.
98. The punishment of the betrayer of a loved one.
99. To enforce a surrender.
100. To avoid banishment.
101. To be avenged upon one who has stolen the affections of a loved one.
102. To escape death.
103. To prevent an agreement's being consummated.
104. Vengeance against one who is guilty of espionage.
105. To escape from custody.
106. Because one covets another's possession.
107. To make an atonement.
108. The desire to escape from a curse.
109. To avoid disqualification.
110. Vengeance against a blackmailer.
111. To escape from a debauch.
112. Escaping from a device.
113. To remove a political obstacle.

THE 'MOTIVE' IS
(Continued)

114. To escape domination.
115. The prevention of a massacre.
116. Vengeance against one who is holding a loved one as hostage.
117. To escape humiliation.
118. To avoid judgment.
119. To protect a loved one, falsely accused.
120. To cause a demonstration.
121. To carry out the terms of a legend or myth.
122. Vengeance against a physical monster.
123. To avoid obedience.
124. The prevention of a panic.
125. To facilitate a discovery.
126. To escape a sentence.
127. To prevent a sacrifice of honor.
128. Vengeance against one who has caused insanity.
129. To conceal embarrassing facts from a loved one.
130. To obtain relief from remorse.
131. The ambition to prove one's honesty.
132. Because one has been "framed".
133. The obtaining of a ransom.
134. The desire to gain possession of a hostage.
135. The ambition to gain prominence.
136. Vengeance against a hypocrite.
137. To prevent exposure.
138. To escape from being a prey.
139. The necessity to obtain food or clothing.
140. To prevent the sacrifice of health.
141. To escape blackmail.
142. Jealous revenge against a rival in love.
143. To escape from tyranny.

THE MOTIVE IS
(Continued)

144. To be rid of carping.
145. The desire to bring about a reformation.
146. To overthrow authority.
147. To escape a foreboding tragedy.
148. Vengeance against one who has caused a miscarriage of justice.
149. To escape ridicule.
150. The demand or the desire to save a life.
151. To escape from an asylum.
152. The desire to obtain a project.
153. Because one has entered into a conspiracy.
154. Vengeance against one who has caused the suicide of a loved one.
155. To escape disgrace.
156. The necessity to take the offensive in a conflict.
157. Vengeance against one who has aroused jealousy.
158. The prevention of malpractice.
159. The desire to gain possession of a valuable.
160. Because one has brought suspicion.
161. Because one has refused mercy.
162. Vengeance against the slanderer of a loved one.
163. To escape from incrimination.
164. One is a victim of auto-suggestion.
165. Because one has refused leniency.
166. To be rid of a repulsive thing.
167. Vengeance against a robber.
168. To retrieve a lost hope.
169. Self defense.
170. To escape severe punishment.
171. Vengeance against one who has insulted his race.
172. To be revenged on one who has broken up home.

THE MOTIVE IS
(Continued)

173. To punish a deserter.
174. To satisfy a depravity.
175. Vengeance against a slanderer.
176. The avoidance of a criminal entanglement.
177. To satisfy an ungovernable temper.
178. Because one has made false statements.
179. To obtain a release of a loved one.
180. Insanely jealous love.

The End.

Wycliffe A. Hill
(1883-1965)

Books by Wycliffe A. Hill

- Ten Million Salable Camera Shots: A Veritable Gold Mine of Ideas for The Amateur Camera Owner

- Plot Genie: Supplementary Formula No. 1. Romance Without Melodrama

- Plot Genie: Supplementary Formula No. 2. Action-Adventure

- Plot Genie: Supplementary Formula No. 3. Detective-Mystery

- Plot Genie: Supplementary Formula No. 4. Comedy

- Plot Genie: Supplementary Formula No. 5. True Confessions

- Plot Genie: Supplementary Formula No. 6. Short-Short Story

- Why Horses Win: An Encyclopedia of Racing, Containing the Results of an Analysis of 1,000 Races and Much Other Valuable Information for the Turf Fan

- Ten Million Photoplay Plots: The Master Key to All Dramatic Plots

- "Debunking The Literary Rackets"

- "The 12 Cardinal Points To Success As A Writer

- How To Choose A Successful Pen Name

CPSIA information can be obtained at www.ICGtesting.com
Printed in the USA
LVOW09s1450130316

478987LV00018B/629/P